WASHINGTON

ART OF THE STATE

ART OF THE STATE

WASHINGTON

The Spirit of America

Text by Nancy Friedman

Harry N. Abrams, Inc., Publishers

NEW YORK

This book was prepared for publication at
Walking Stick Press, San Francisco

Project staff:
    Series Designer: Linda Herman
    Series Editor: Diana Landau

For Harry N. Abrams, Inc.:
    Series Editor: Ruth A. Peltason

Page 1: *Birling* (log-rolling contest) by Robert Chamberlain, c. 1980s.
    Courtesy the artist

Page 2: Nez Perce cornhusk bag with woven evergreen tree design, c. 1900.
    American Hurrah Archive, New York

Library of Congress Cataloging-in-Publication Data

Friedman, Nancy.
    Washington : the spirit of America, state by state / by Nancy Friedman.
        p.   cm. — (Art of the state)
    Includes bibliographical references and index.
    ISBN 0–8109–5559–8
    1. Washington (State)—Civilization—Pictorial works.
2. Washington (State)—Miscellanea.   I. Title.   II. Series.
F892.F75   1999
979.7—dc21   98–43105

Harry N. Abrams, Inc.
100 Fifth Avenue
New York, N.Y. 10011
www.abramsbooks.com

Red Chair by Joel Brock, 1998. *Lisa Harris Gallery, Seattle*

CONTENTS

Untitled (Shipyards at Dockton, Maury Island) by Alice Samson, c. 1907. *Museum of History and Industry, Seattle*

> *"The Evergreen Land is a place to which you come, not a place from which you escape."*
>
> Nard Jones, Evergreen Land, *1947*

People have been coming to the land of the Columbia and the Cascades for some 12,000 years, and for most of that time Washington seemed impossibly remote and raw, majestic and forbidding. Its shoreline and rivers defied navigation, its glacier-clad mountains paradoxically spewed steam, and its vast forests appeared impenetrable. "It is the farthest reach in the broad land," wrote Nard Jones of his native state shortly after World War II, "and when you arrive you cannot separate yourself further from the older regions of home." Settlers were tempted by the land's bounty and daunted by its challenges. Survival—staying one step ahead of nature—was the paramount goal. Compared with even the rest of the Far West, territorial status came late here; so did statehood, railroads, and the arts.

Yet from the beginning, the landscape's sheer dynamism inspired in Washingtonians a comparable vitality. This is a land where big gestures and upstart attitudes seem appropriate. The potlatches of the coastal Natives— elaborate ceremonies in which huge quantities of possessions were given away, proving the giver's wealth—could have occurred nowhere else in America, because no other indigenous people enjoyed such casual affluence. Washington's first American emigrants were unusual too: for one thing, they included several people of African descent who had migrated northward because Oregon law forbade African-American settlement. One, a former slave named George Washington, founded the town of Centralia.

Washington gave birth to Boeing's jumbo jets, to Grand Coulee's jumbo dam, and to jumbo tycoons like Bill Gates, founder of the Microsoft empire. Even legends are outsized here, from Sasquatch (a.k.a. Bigfoot) to Paul Bunyan to "flying saucers"—so named by their first reported observer, a pilot who flew over Mount Rainier in 1947.

Washington has been home to large-scale political and social ideals as well. Utopian communities flourished here in the late 19th century. Women were able to vote by the 1870s, when Washington was still a territory. The labor movement was so vigorous—and so radical—that it was able to organize the nation's first general strike in 1919. Idealism had its dark side, though, in violent campaigns against the Native and Chinese populations.

While Washington's men were felling forests and lobbying for railroads, women were quietly building the state's cultural life. Late-19th-century

Detail of Arctic Building, Seattle.
Photo Wolfgang Kaehler

artistic pioneers included painters like Abby Williams Hill, whose landscapes were commissioned by the state and the railroads, and Harriet Foster Beecher, who painted portraits, Puget Sound seascapes, and still lifes. Women founded the Tacoma Art League and the Seattle Art School and mounted the state's first art competitions and exhibitions. And they took an equally important role in the nonvisual arts, as poets, journalists, and musicians; one Madame Davenport Engberg, who commanded the podium in 1914 during an orchestra performance in Bellingham, was the world's first female conductor.

World War II propelled Washington onto center stage in the national drama. While Boeing was turning out fighter planes in Everett, a secret nuclear plant in Hanford was creating plutonium for the bomb that would be dropped on Nagasaki. There was much

"The Apple Family" promotional postcard, 1910. *Special Collections Division, University of Washington Libraries*

upheaval in the arts as well. The painters of the Northwest School—Mark Tobey, Morris Graves, Kenneth Callahan, and Guy Anderson—attracted international attention with paintings that merged Asian symbolism with regional subjects. Shortly after the war, Theodore Roethke arrived at the University of Washington and began to inspire a generation of major regional poets. By the 1970s, Washington boasted a vibrant cultural scene that included important institutions in music, theater, and dance.

Today, Washington continues to go its own way with dash and vigor. High technology vies with traditional resource industries for economic preeminence, and the combination of outdoor pursuits and a sophisticated cultural landscape earns the state top ratings for livability. An increasingly diverse population, enriched by Hispanic and Asian communities, shapes a cosmopolitan outlook befitting this state on the upper edge of the nation. The closest point to Asia in the lower 48 states, Washington looks across the Pacific toward a global frontier. ♣

WASHINGTON

"The Evergreen State"
42nd State

Date of Statehood
NOVEMBER 11, 1889

Capital
OLYMPIA

Bird
WILLOW GOLDFINCH

Flower
COAST RHODODENDRON

Tree
WESTERN HEMLOCK

Fish
STEELHEAD TROUT

Animal
ROOSEVELT ELK

Fruit
APPLE

Washington's official symbols speak of wilderness and cultivation, of controversy and sheer cussedness. "Washington" itself was a compromise; many settlers preferred "Columbia," after the mighty river that defines the state, but bowed to protests from the District of Columbia and named their territory for the nation's first president. The Evergreen State had no official tree until 1946, when an Oregon newspaper high-handedly chose the western hemlock for its neighbor. Indignant Washington newspapers named their own tree, the western red cedar, until a legislator defended the hemlock as the future "backbone of the state's forest industry." (He was right.) The willow goldfinch actually lost in a schoolchildren's contest for state bird, earning its title only because seven other states had already

Willow goldfinch and coast rhododendron

State seal

"Alki" (By and by)

State motto, a Chinook expression

claimed the meadowlark. Even the state motto—the only one in a Native language—mixes irony and optimism. Early settlers in what became Seattle named their village "New York Alki," hoping that "by and by" their remote outpost would become a civilized metropolis. ♣

Above: A steelhead trout (*Salmo gairdnerii*) leaps up a waterfall. The steelhead is a seagoing variety of rainbow trout. *Photo Tom and Pat Leeson/Weststock Right:* A decorative stamp, c. 1930s, conveys the "apple a day" message. *Private collection*

EAT
WASHINGTON
STATE
APPLES *for Health*

Above: Ruddy of cheek, robust of physique, and posed against a scenic backdrop of river and mountain, the "Washington Belle" embodied the wholesome qualities of life in the Evergreen State. This postcard was printed around 1909. *Private collection*

Planked Salmon

Washington's coastal Makah and S'Kallam Indians developed this traditional preparation, still one of the finest ways to cook salmon. Cedar imparts the best flavor, but any untreated wood will do—even driftwood. Curing the wood with wine is a contemporary flourish; for a regional flavor, use a Washington State Pinot Noir.

To fireproof the wooden plank, soak in a mixture of 1 part red wine and 2 parts water at least 1 hour and up to 1 day. Filet a whole salmon and rub with rock salt, brown sugar, and white pepper; cover and chill 2 to 4 hours. Rinse and pat dry. Using 22-gauge (or heavier) wire, securely lash salmon to the plank. Prop plank over hot coals at a 45-degree angle, 1½ to 2 feet from heat. Cook until surface turns evenly opaque, 20 to 30 minutes, basting several times with a butter-lemon juice mixture. Carefully rotate plank so skin faces the heat and cook 20 to 30 minutes more, basting several times. To serve, lay fish on a platter, snip wires, and gently pull plank away.

Adapted from several sources

Forever Plaid

Washington is the only state that claims an official tartan. Designed in 1988 by two country dancers from Vancouver, the Evergreen State tartan has a forest-green background with bands of blue (representing lakes, rivers, and ocean), white (for snow-capped mountains), red (for apples and cherries), yellow (for wheat), and black (for the eruption of Mount St. Helens).

Above: When it was built in 1920, the state capitol building in Olympia was the fourth-highest dome in the world. *Photo Kirkendall & Spring/ Weststock. Left:* Roosevelt elk (*Cervus canadensis occidentalis*), also known as Olympic elk. Largest of the wapiti, these majestic creatures roam in large herds on the Olympic Peninsula. *Photo Tom & Pat Leeson/Photo Researchers, Inc.*

"Washington, My Home"

Our verdant forest green
Caressed by silv'ry stream
From mountain peak
To fields of wheat
Washington, my home.

*Verse from the official state song,
words and music by Helen Davis*

"Roll On, Columbia"

In 1941, a 28-year-old folksinger
named Woody Guthrie came to the Northwest
to write songs for a film promoting public power and
Columbia River development. In 30 days Guthrie
wrote 26 songs, for which he was paid $270. Among
them was "Roll On, Columbia," named the official
Washington State folk song in 1987.

Rhododendron Rules

When Washington needed
floral representation at the
1892 Chicago World's Fair,
only women were allowed
to vote for the state's official
flower. The contest came
down to the native coast
rhododendron versus the common clover. The "rhodie" barely
won with just 53 percent of the
vote. Western Washington is
prime rhododendron country;
about 500 pure species are hardy
to the climate, and there are
many more greenhouse varieties.
Whidbey Island's mild year-round
climate makes it one of the best
spots in the state to see wild
rhododendrons.

(to the tune of "Good Night, Irene")
Roll on, Columbia, roll on,
Roll on, Columbia, roll on,
Your power is turning our darkness to dawn.
So roll on, Columbia, roll on.

*Above: Rhododendron by Paul
De Longpre. Native to Washington, the coast rhododendron
is ubiquitous in both wild and
cultivated varieties. Christie's
Images. Left:* Roots of a mature
hemlock tree in the Olympic
rainforest. With annual rainfall
of as much as 200 inches, the
Olympic Peninsula supports
vast stands of hemlocks as well
as Sitka spruce, Douglas fir, and
Western red cedar. *Photo Tom
and Pat Leeson/Weststock*

1579 Pacific Northwest coast skirted by Francis Drake and claimed for Great Britain.

1592 Juan de Fuca's legendary discovery of strait between Vancouver Island and Olympic Peninsula.

1775 Coast claimed for Spain by Bruno Heceta and Juan Francisco de Bodega.

1778 Seeking the fabled Northwest Passage, Capt. James Cook skirts the Northwest coast but misses mouth of the Columbia.

1787 Capt. Charles Barkley enters and names the Strait of Juan de Fuca.

1792 Columbia River discovered by Capt. Robert Gray; Puget Sound claimed for Great Britain by Capt. George Vancouver.

1805 Meriwether Lewis and William Clark complete their 4,000-mile cross-country trek by descending the Columbia River to the Pacific Ocean.

1810 First trading outpost established by North West Fur Company.

1818 North West Company establishes Fort Walla Walla.

1819 Spain cedes its Northwest claims to the United States.

1821 North West and Hudson's Bay Companies merge.

1832 First American overland party arrives at Fort Vancouver.

1836 Dr. Marcus Whitman establishes Waiilatpu Mission near Walla Walla.

1843 First major American emigration to Northwest.

1845 First American settlement, in Tumwater.

1846 U.S.–Canadian boundary fixed at 49 degrees north.

1847 Whitman massacre.

1853 Washington Territory created from Oregon Territory. Population 3,965.

1855 Widespread Indian uprisings follow attempt to remove tribes to reservations.

1859 Gold rush in eastern Washington.

1860 Population 11,594.

1861 Territorial University (now University of Washington) opens in Seattle.

1863 Eastern boundary of Washington established, following creation of Idaho Territory.

1880 Population 75,116.

1883 Northern Pacific Railroad from Great Lakes to Puget Sound completed via Columbia River route.

1889 Washington admitted as 42nd state. Great Seattle fire.

1890 Population 336,232.

1893 Great Northern Railroad completed to Seattle.

1899 Mount Rainier National Park created.

1900 Population 518,103.

1901 First movie theater built in Seattle.

1903 Seattle Symphony founded.

1906 Washington State Art Association founded.

1907 Industrial Workers of the World (Wobblies) organized.

1909 Alaska-Yukon-Pacific Exposition.

1910 Washington voters approve women's suffrage, nine years before U.S. Congress approves 19th Amendment. Population 1,141,990.

1914 Cornish School of Allied Arts founded; curriculum includes visual arts, music, and dance.

1916 Transcontinental telephone service extended to Seattle.

1919 Armed conflict between Wobblies and American Legion; general strike in Seattle.

1928 State capitol at Olympia completed.

1933 Seattle Art Museum opens.

1934 General strike in Seattle.

1938 Olympic National Park created.

1940 Population 1,736,191.

1941 Main structure of Grand Coulee Dam completed.

1943 The Hanford Project started, to produce plutonium for an atomic bomb.

1960 Population 2,853,214.

1962 "Century 21," the Seattle World's Fair, runs from April through October.

1974 Expo 74 opens in Spokane.

1980 Mount St. Helens erupts on May 18, blanketing much of eastern Washington in volcanic ash.

1990 Population 5,240,900.

1991 Seattle Art Museum moves to new downtown building created by architect Robert Venturi.

1998 Benaroya Hall, new home of the Seattle Symphony, opens after 12 years of planning and construction.

Its generally mild climate can be deceptive: Lying between the 45th and 49th parallels, Washington is the northernmost state besides Alaska. Bellingham is considerably farther north than Bangor, Maine; Seattle is more northerly than Halifax, Nova Scotia. When traveling to Washington in the winter, take into account the shorter days.

Washington's spectacular terrain is a clamor of contrasts: glaciers and volcanoes, rainforest and sagebrush, canyons and plateaus. The earth here was born in violent continental clashes that rocked the ocean bed, expelled huge flows of molten basalt, and thrust four great mountain ranges—the Cascades, the Olympics, the Blues, and the Columbias—thousands of feet into the sky. This is young country, geologically speaking—200 million years ago the entire state lay

submerged beneath the Pacific Ocean—and it displays the dramatic moods of adolescence. The Cascade Range, a chain of volcanic mountains, bisects the state, dividing the rain-sodden west from the semiarid east. Blocking the energy of Pacific storms, the range creates a huge rain shadow; thus the Olympic Peninsula gets up to 200 inches of rain and snow per year, while the Palouse hills in the east average only 7 to 15 inches. ♣

"WITHIN A SINGLE SWEEP OF VISION WERE SEVEN SNOW-peaks…I cannot express their vague, yet vast and intense splendor, by any other word than incandescence. It was as if the sky had suddenly grown white-hot in patches."

Fitz Hugh Ludlow, in The Atlantic Monthly, *1864. Ludlow was a New Yorker whose traveling companion in the West was the painter Albert Bierstadt.*

At 14,410 feet, Mount Rainier is Washington's highest point and one of its most striking landmarks. A dormant volcano that last erupted about 150 years ago, it is capped by year-round ice and shrouded in the largest single-peak glacial system in the continental United States. The Klickitat Indians called it "Ta-kho-ma"—"The Mountain"—and believed it was inhabited by an angry god. In 1792, British Captain George Vancouver glimpsed the mountain from Puget Sound and named it for a fellow naval officer, Peter Rainier, who never laid eyes on his namesake. The mountain and its surroundings became the fifth national park in 1899, the result of a land swap between the Northern Pacific Railroad and the U.S. government.

Phases of Rainier

Ghost
Afloat
In the most lost
Time: omitted remote
Acts of love: unaccounted cost:
Old thinking cap: pearl-sailed, swan-swaddled boat:
Egret of plunge and plume: scarred, flaw-flushed, embossed...

Nelson Bentley, 1966

Opposite: Mount Rainier by Lionel E. Salmon, 1938. Washington State Historical Society, Tacoma Above: One of the mountain's many picturesque alpine meadows. *Photo Art Wolfe. Left:* Modern dancers in Paradise Valley in the 1920s. *Underwood Photo Archives, San Francisco.* The highest peak in the Cascade Range, which runs from southwestern Canada through northern California, Mount Rainier has inspired artists in every medium. The mountain is open year-round for hiking, skiing, climbing, and enjoying breathtaking views.

> *"Rain falling in torrents—we are all wet as usial [sic]."*
>
> William Clark, from the journals of Meriwether Lewis and William Clark,
> November 11, 1805

Water, Water Everywhere

Water in every form—descending from the peaks, swirling in the ocean, pouring from the heavens—gives Washington a distinctly aqueous cast. Some of North America's greatest rivers traverse the state, including the mighty Columbia, 1,214 miles long and nearly 10 miles wide near the Pacific Ocean. No river on the continent travels faster,

descending 1,200 feet in 600 miles. Tumbling through deep gorges, the Columbia and its tributaries—the Snake, the Pend Oreille, the Spokane, the Yakima, and more—create spectacular waterfalls with names like Cascade, Fairy, Horseshoe, and Klickitat. More than 8,000 natural lakes dot the landscape, as well as the world's second-largest manmade lake. Washington's coast is an intricate maze of bays, straits, and sounds, thronged with islands—most notably the San Juans, an archipelago of 172 named isles—stretching the shoreline to more than 1,800 miles. Harbor seals, sea lions, Dall's porpoises, orcas, and gray whales live along the coast permanently or seasonally, as do five species of salmon and the geoduck, a huge native clam.

...the waves coming forward, without cessation,
The waves, altered by sand-bars, beds of kelp,
    miscellaneous driftwood,
Topped by cross-winds, tugged at by sinuous
    undercurrents
The tide rustling in, sliding between the ridges of stone,
The tongues of water, creeping in, quietly....

Theodore Roethke, "Meditation at Oyster River," 1966

Above: Panoramic View of Olympic Mountains by Emily Inez Denny, 1894. *Museum of History and Industry, Seattle. Opposite above:* Breaching orca near San Juan Island. The San Juans are home to three resident pods of *Orcinus orca,* also known as "killer" whales. From May to September whales can often be spotted from shore. *Photo F. Stuart Westmorland Opposite below:* Rainforest streams in Olympic National Park. *Photo Art Wolfe*

How Wet Is It?

True, in 1898 a boy drowned on a Seattle street. True, the Olympic Peninsula is one of the wettest places on the planet. But deluges are the exception; steady drizzle (with occasional "sun breaks," as they're known locally) is the rule in most of Washington. With average annual precipitation of about 34 inches, most of it in the winter months, Seattle actually gets less rainfall than Miami, New Orleans, or New York City.

Deep Lake, Scabland Channel, near Grand Coulee. The Channeled Scablands were created by glacial melt at the end of the last ice age, about 10,000 years ago. The ice carved deep canyons, or coulees— the two largest are Grand Coulee and Moses Coulee—and left a nearly barren lava plateau. *Photo Gary Braasch*

Inland Empire

East of the Cascades lie the Okanogan Highlands and the Columbia Plateau, comprising arid badlands, scablands formed by Ice Age floods, and irrigated wheat fields and orchards. This is the northernmost part of the Great American Desert, which covers much of the West from here to Arizona. Ponderosa pine forests cover rolling hillsides formed by basalt lava flows; ship-shaped rocks and mesas point to the northeast, suggesting the direction of massive flooding about 20,000 years ago. Giant boulders known as "haystacks," deposited during an ice age more than a million years ago, punctuate the terrain. Temperatures here are much more extreme than in the wet western half of the state, with summer days reaching 100 degrees and January daytime highs around 30 degrees. Although mined extensively in the 19th century, today the region's treasure is agricultural, thanks to the extensive irrigation system created by damming the Columbia River.

Deep Lake, Scabland Channel, near Grand Coulee. The Channeled Scablands were created by glacial melt at the end of the last ice age, about 10,000 years ago. The ice carved deep canyons, or coulees— the two largest are Grand Coulee and Moses Coulee—and left a nearly barren lava plateau. *Photo Gary Braasch*

"THE EAST SIDE [OF THE CASCADES], THE SIDE with the desert, the dams, the irrigation ditches…is like every other part of the West. Too dry for comfort, always jealous of the living it wrests from the river."

Blaine Harden, A River Lost:
The Life and Death of the Columbia, *1996*

"EVERYONE KNEW THAT SAND WOULD GROW JUST AS GOOD orchards as any other soil if you got it wet....We set out trees, built houses, formed a local improvement district... and saw a bright vision,"

Okanogan Valley settler, 1907

Spring wheatfields in the Palouse, eastern Washington. Massive irrigation projects have transformed barren volcanic soil into agricultural wonders. *Photo F. Stuart Westmorland*

In 1850, an emigrant from Iowa carefully nurtured a fir seedling on his long journey across the plains to Washington; he didn't want to be lonesome for evergreens, he said. He needn't have taken such pains. Forests cover more than half of the Evergreen State—primarily Douglas fir west of the Cascades and ponderosa pines in the east. The state is home to some of the world's biggest trees, including the largest known western hemlock, Douglas fir, Sitka spruce, and red alder. Even after extensive 19th-century logging, about 15 percent of the state remains old-growth forest (more than 250 years old). The dense stands of timber shelter many large mammals, including the Roosevelt elk, black bears, mountain goats, cougars, and red fox. Up in the forest canopy live crows, ravens, western tanagers, bald eagles, and the endangered spotted owl. ♣

"THE FIRS WERE EVERYWHERE, BIG AND VIRILE, WITH THEIR strong roots pulling all of the vitality out of the soil and leaving the poor little fruit trees only enough food and light to keep an occasional branch alive. These were no kin to the neatly spaced little Christmas tree ladies of the back pasture. These were fierce invaders. Pillagers and rapers."

Betty MacDonald, The Egg and I, *1945. MacDonald and her husband moved to the Olympic Peninsula in the early 1930s to start a chicken ranch.*

"GO LOOK AT THE TALLEST TREE IN THE EAST; IMAGINE IT THREE times as tall. Imagine that all about you are trees like that with their crowns interlocking till they shut out the sky. Imagine their trunks so close together that one cannot see more than a few rods into the forest.... Imagine this forest going on... unbroken over a stretch of about two hundred thousand acres."

Donald Culross Peattie, in Audubon *magazine, 1941*

Opposite: Pines by Edgar Forkner, c. 1911–20. *Henry Art Gallery, University of Washington Above:* Great horned owlet, North Cascades National Park. *Photo Art Wolfe. Left:* Hoh Rainforest, Olympic National Park. In 1897, a ranger for the new park defended protecting the ancient trees: "They say they are...overripe... and some of them will fall down. Some of them will keep on falling down and others will take their place in the process which has gone on for a thousand years...." *Photo Mark Newman*

The Belle of the Yakimas. Photographed by Frank LaRoche, 1899. *Library of Congress. Opposite above: Scene on the Columbia River* by John Mix Stanley, c. 1852. *Amon Carter Museum, Fort Worth, Texas. Opposite below:* Petroglyphs (possibly Makah or Quileute) near Sand Point, Olympic National Park. *Photo Cindy McIntyre/Weststock*

Washington's first inhabitants arrived about 12,000 years ago, at the end of the last ice age. Those who settled on the coast established a culture unique among North American Natives for its wealth and stability. These Coast Salish, Chinook, Clallam, Clatsop, Makah, Lummi, and other groups lived in clans—villages of extended families—rather than tribes. Their huge cedar "long houses" were the largest buildings on the continent (some were 100 feet long, divided into eight or ten rooms), and their cedar canoes were beautifully carved using only stone and wooden tools. Their ceremonial "potlatches," in which huge numbers of belongings were given away or burned, were elaborate displays of (literally) disposable wealth.

On the dry plateaus east of the Cascades, life was much harsher for the scattered, seminomadic groups of Okanogan, Spokane, Wenatche, Yakama (Yakima), and Nez Perce. Their dwellings were pit-houses six to seven feet underground, or portable twig-and-pole structures; their diets often included rodents and grasshoppers. The most fortunate of the inland peoples were those near the Columbia Gorge, who built platforms over the falls to catch spawning salmon—as many as 500 a day. ⚑

"*God created this Indian country*
and it was like he spread out a big blanket. He put
the Indians on it. They were created here in this
country, truly and honestly, and that was the
time this river started to run."

Chief Meninock, Yakima Nation, 1915

A Chinook Lexicon

Bostons	Americans
chuck	water
cultus	worthless
hyas	great, very
illahee	land
kalakala	bird
King Chautsh	English
klahanie	outdoors
klootchman	woman
kloshe	good, fine
la tet	head
melamoose	dead
moos-moos	cattle
muckamuck	food, eat
siwash	Indian
skookum	strong, big
tillakum	friend
tyee	chief

Chinook Jargon

By the time Europeans arrived, the Tsinuk (Chinook) Indians of the lower banks of the Columbia River were the region's foremost traders, and an argot based on their language was the lingua franca throughout the Pacific Northwest. Augmented by French and English, Chinook jargon became the common language of Washington pioneers throughout the 19th century and into the 20th. One term even entered everyday Americanese: "high muckamuck," meaning "much food," and, by extension, "important person."

Above: **Beaded bags from the Plateau cultural area, c. 1850–1925.** *Washington State Historical Society.* **Left: T'cayas.** **Soft-twined basket with design of wolves and salmon gills. Twana (Snokomish), c. 1910.** *Seattle Art Museum. Photo Paul Macapia*

Left: Detail of a Salish-style totem pole carved by Carol Batdorf at the Tennant Lake Interpretive Center in Ferndale, c. 1979. *Photo Steve Solum/Weststock. Below:* Wishxam totem by Lillian Pitt, 1995. Pitt, whose tribal heritage is Warm Spring, Wasco, and Wishxam, is known for her fired clay masks and mixed-media sculptures on themes drawn from legends of the Columbia River peoples. This piece incorporates wood and anagama-fired clay—a very slow, hot firing process based on an 8th-century Korean method. Pitt uses one of only two such kilns in the U.S. for her work, which she calls "subconscious portraiture." *Courtesy the artist*

Totem Poles

Although not native to Washington (they originated farther north, in British Columbia and the Queen Charlotte Islands), totem poles became a distinctive part of the Washington landscape well before statehood. They are especially plentiful in Seattle, symbolizing that city's role as Gateway to the North. Originally used as memorials to the dead or as architectural supports, totem poles incorporated mythological figures such as Raven, Frog, and Coyote. The top position goes to the symbol of the clan whose story is being told.

A View in Coal Harbour, in Cook's River, 1786. Engraving of a drawing by Joseph Woodcock. Pacific Northwest Collection, University of Washington Libraries

A Passage to the Pacific

The quest for the fabled Northwest Passage—the inland waterway linking the Atlantic and Pacific Oceans—drew Spanish and English navigators to the Washington coast in the late 18th century. (An account of a 16th-century exploration by the Greek mariner known as Juan de Fuca—for whom the Washington strait is named—is probably spurious.) Captain James Cook wrote one of the first credible descriptions of the coast, and Captain George Vancouver named many prominent landmarks, including Puget Sound and Mount Rainier. But it was a fur trader from Boston, Captain Robert Gray, who almost accidentally discovered the mouth of the

Columbia River in 1792 and named it after his ship. His discovery would prove to be the real "Northwest Passage," opening trade and travel from far inland to the Pacific.

"WE COUNTED OVER A HUNDRED CANOES AT ONE TIME, which might be supposed to contain, at an average, five persons each, for few of them had less than three on board; great numbers had seven, eight or nine; and one was manned with no less than seventeen....If they had any distrust or fear of us at first, they now appeared to have laid it aside, for they came on board the ships and mixed with our people with the greatest freedom."

Captain James Cook, on arriving in Nootka Sound in 1778

Above: Early Wedgwood medallion of Captain Cook, c. early 19th century. *Honolulu Academy of Art.* Cook reached the Oregon coast in 1778 and sailed past Washington on his way to Nootka Sound. *Left: Lewis and Clark on the Lower Columbia* by Charles M. Russell, 1905. *Amon Carter Museum, Fort Worth*

Battle of Seattle by Emily Inez Denny, c. 1876–1918. On January 26, 1856, Klickitat Indians crossed Snoqualmie Pass and attacked the city. *Museum of History and Industry, Seattle*

Sent by President Jefferson on a "literary expedition" after the Louisiana Purchase brought the Far West under American administration, Meriwether Lewis and William Clark traveled down the Columbia River to the Pacific in 1805, making detailed notes on the terrain and its inhabitants. Their reports encouraged the Pacific Fur Company to establish forts in Okanogan and Spokane, where it competed with Britain's Hudson's Bay

Company. By the 1830s, the "Oregon country"—present-day Oregon, Washington, Idaho, and parts of Montana and Wyoming—had begun to attract American missionaries, and in 1843 the first 900 pioneers reached southern Washington by way of the Oregon Trail. A decade later, there were enough settlers north of the Columbia River to warrant establishing a separate Washington Territory, with its capital in Olympia. ♣

"Great joy in camp

we are in view of the oceian, this great Pacific Octean which we been so long anxious to See, and the roreing or noise made by the waves brakcing on the rockey Shores (as I suppose) may be heard disti[n]ctly."

Journal of William Clark, November 7, 1805. According to journal editor Bernard De Voto, Clark was mistaken. His camp was near Pillar Rock, and the ocean can't be seen from there.

The Mercer Girls

By 1861 Seattle had a population of about 200, a territorial university, and a conspicuous shortage of women. Asa Shinn Mercer, the university's 22-year-old president, set about to remedy the situation. He made two arduous trips east, bringing 11 ladies back "around the Horn" the first time and 46 the second. All except one of the "Mercer Girls" were married almost as soon as they disembarked; Mercer himself married one of them. The effort paid off in brisk population growth.

Above: Mrs. Thomas Russell née Sarah Gallagher, a Mercer girl. Photograph by Josiah G. Hunter. *Left:* A swivel-mounted gun used at Fort Nisqually, c. 1830. *Both, Washington State Historical Society, Tacoma*

The arrival of the transcontinental railroad in 1883 triggered three decades of explosive growth. Statehood was granted in 1889, but four years later Washington was wracked by a devastating economic depression. In the rush to build the railroad, huge fortunes—and debts—had been accumulated. But the federal treasury, which had switched in 1890 to the silver standard, was running perilously short on gold reserves. A run on banks in the East had devastating repercussions in the West. In Washington, thousands of workers were suddenly unemployed, forced to dig clams and sell cedar shakes to survive. Not until the Klondike gold strike in 1897 would the state recover from its paralysis. ♣

Gateway to Gold

On July 15, 1897, the steamship *Excelsior* arrived in San Francisco carrying prospectors from the Yukon—and a fortune in gold nuggets from Klondike Creek. Two days later the steamer *Portland* reached Seattle with a ton and a half of gold, and the rush was on. An enterprising newspaper editor, Erastus Brainerd, bombarded the nation with news of Seattle's virtues, and the nation took note. For nearly a decade Seattle was the place to buy gear and food for the Yukon adventure, the place to weigh and sell the gold shipped back from the Klondike, and the place to buy more supplies for the return trip.

"GOLD SEEKERS TUMBLED OUT OF EVERY NORTHERN Pacific and Great Northern train and out of every Sound steamer: pale bookkeepers and brown farm hands and pursy businessmen; self-conscious young men with determined young wives who believed that wealth is as much a woman's business as a man's; unsuccessful lawyers, undertakers and prostitutes.... There were also miners among them."

Archie Binns, Northwest Gateway, *1941*

Above: View of Seattle from the Bay by Charles Graham, illustration from Harper's Weekly, *c. 1890s. San Francisco Public Library. Left: Trains linked the coal-mining town of Franklin to Seattle in the late 1890s. Museum of History and Industry, Seattle. Opposite: Prospector bringing in supplies on Dead Horse Trail, 1897. Washington State Historical Society*

Tug Echo and Raft by Robert Chamberlain, 1989. Logs were rafted together and towed upriver to sawmills. *Courtesy the artist. Below:* Advertising art for Durable Douglas Fir by Bror Leonard Crondal, 1926. *Washington State Historical Society, Tacoma. Opposite:* 25-foot-high statue of Paul Bunyan in Puyallup. *Photo Harry Whitmore*

Durable Douglas Fir *America's Permanent Lumber Supply*

"*Timber is a crop.*"

Weyerhaeuser slogan, 1930s

From Timber to Lumber

Douglas fir, hemlock, spruce, cedar—Washington's vast forests were seen by early settlers as a virtually limitless resource. The land around Puget Sound, in particular, was "a lumber-man's paradise," wrote one observer. After the California gold discovery in 1848, lumberyards sprouted up all along the Sound, turning out building supplies for the burgeoning city of San Francisco. Within a decade, Washington sawmills also shipped lumber to Honolulu and the Hawaiian

The legend of Paul Bunyan, the larger-than-life lumberjack and folk hero, was born in the lumber camps of the Great Lakes/Canadian border area, but moved west with the migrant loggers who invented the tales. The first published collection of Paul Bunyan stories was written in 1925 by Iowa-born James Stevens, who worked his way to Washington as a poet, singer, soldier, and logger.

sugar plantations, and to more far-flung Pacific ports as well. Railroads opened the eastern states to Washington lumber and made Everett, at the mouth of the Snohomish River, a town of millionaires. Chief among them was German-born Frederick Weyerhaeuser, who came west from Minnesota to create the timber empire that still bears his name.

Today Washington ranks second, after Oregon, in lumber production. The forests were overlogged in the 1980s, and many mills closed; in the 1990s, controversy over endangered species—especially the spotted owl—focused attention on the dwindling old-growth forests.

Riches from River and Sea

Washington's native people on both sides of the Cascades had long relied on the region's abundant marine and river life for survival and trade. By the 1860s, later settlers had created a salmon industry based on new fishing and canning techniques. Where Natives had spearfished from platforms high above the Columbia, catching salmon as they battled upriver to spawn, white emigrants devised huge nets to harvest Chinook and coho salmon farther downstream, or in the waters around the San Juan Islands. Extensive damming of the Columbia in the mid-20th century barred salmon from their spawning ground, and their numbers declined dramatically. Oystering also has been important since long before statehood. Native Americans used dried

Above: Poster advertising canned salmon from *The Salmon Canning Industry* by Ernest D. Clark and Ray W. Clough, 1926. The invention of the tin can allowed Columbia River salmon to be shipped around the world. *Washington State Historical Society, Tacoma. Right:* Harvesting oysters on Willapa Bay. *Photo Charles R. Pearson. Opposite: Fish Migration* by Gaylen Hansen, 1996–97. *Linda Hodges Gallery*

Willapa Bay oysters as currency, and bayside towns from Oysterville to Long Beach were literally built on oyster shells. Overharvesting decimated the native bivalves by the 1880s; not until the introduction of Japanese species did Washington's oyster industry begin to recover.

"THE IMMENSE NUMBERS OF ALL KINDS OF SALMON WHICH ASCEND the Columbia annually is something wonderful. They seem to be seeking quiet and safe places to deposit their spawn and thousands of them never stop until they can reach the great falls of the Snake River, more than 600 miles from the sea."

Frances Fuller Victor, All Over Oregon & Washington, 1872

A Farming Cornucopia

Until the "miracle" of irrigation, farming in Washington was problematic. West of the Cascades the land was too wet and heavily forested for silage crops; east of the mountains it was parched and barren. Private irrigation projects in the 1870s transformed the Yakima Valley from ranchland to farmland; the rich volcanic soil needed only the blessing of water to yield bumper crops of cherries, apples, hops, asparagus, and pears. Farther east, in the Palouse (a French word meaning "lawn"), 100-foot-deep soils produce more wheat per acre than any other dryland farming area, and Walla Walla lays claim to some of the world's sweetest onions. Since the 1970s premium wine grapes have become a growth industry: the Yakima and Columbia valleys lie at the same latitude as France's Burgundy and Loire regions, and produce world-class Cabernet Sauvignon, Pinot Noir, Chardonnay, and Riesling. Growing tulips is big business, too: the Skagit River Valley produces more bulbs than Holland.

Left: This altered photograph of "giant grapes" by Asahel Curtis promoted Washington's agricultural bounty, 1913. *Washington State Historical Society, Tacoma Above: Fields of Gold* by Alfred Currier, 1996. *Courtesy the artist. Opposite:* Washington apple crate label, c. 1920s. *Private collection.* Apples are the state's best-known crop by far. From seeds planted at Hudson's Bay Company forts in the early 1800s, production has grown to 60 percent of the nation's total—with emphasis on the Red Delicious variety.

"Below us throbbed the wheat.

This is undulating country, and the wheat, planted along the hills in eccentric rings and ovals, climbs up one slope and down another. We were flying very low, and the tops of the wheat were intermittently touched by wind; it looked as if somebody were running a gentle invisible thumb over orange plush."

John Gunther, Inside USA, *1947*

High-Flyers to High Tech

Washington has made a stunningly successful and rapid transition from the resource industries of forestry, fishing, and agriculture to a knowledge- and technology-based economy. Two homegrown companies, Boeing and Microsoft, epitomize the change. The state's largest employer and one of the most innovative aircraft companies anywhere, Boeing began producing military planes during World War I and made its reputation with the B-17 bomber during World War II. Its 707 airplane was the first jet-powered passenger plane, and its plant, built in Everett in the late 1960s, is the world's largest production facility. Microsoft, founded in 1979 by young computer programmers Bill Gates and Paul Allen, built a software empire on the

Above: One of the intricate, inventive screens of the popular interactive game "Riven," copyright 1997. *Courtesy Cyan, Inc. Right:* The Great Gallery of the Museum of Flight in Seattle. More than 40 aircraft—from Boeing's first plane to the Apollo spacecraft—are displayed in the immense space. *Museum of Flight, Seattle. Photo F. Stuart Westmorland*

platform of MS-DOS, once the universal operating system for personal computers. Now headquartered in Redmond, Microsoft paved the way for dozens of other Washington-based computer companies, including Aldus, creator of the desktop publishing program PageMaker; and Cyan, developer of the popular interactive games "Myst" and "Riven."

"I WAS ON EDGE THE WHOLE TIME THINKING, 'Will this thing be fast enough? Will somebody come along and do it faster?'"

Bill Gates, quoted in Programmers at Work, *1986*

Above: Microsoft headquarters in Redmond. The "campus," virtual home to more than 14,000 employees, comprises 32 buildings on 263 acres. *Photo Tim Heneghan/Weststock Left:* Luggage tag, c. 1930, from the Boeing Company. *Courtesy the Boeing Company Historical Archives*

Marcus Whitman and his party at South Pass, 1836. Artist unknown. Corbis-Bettmann

Beginning in the early 1800s, Roman Catholic and Protestant missionaries vied for the souls of Washington's Natives, who were deemed atheists in desperate need of salvation. Catholic priests, unencumbered by families, had a slight advantage: for several years Congregationalist clergy had to be shipped over from Honolulu, the nearest missionary station. By the late 1820s, stories of godless Northwest Indians reached the East

Coast, and many missionaries heeded the call. Among them were Dr. Marcus Whitman and his wife, Narcissa, who established a mission at Waiilatpu ("the place of the people of the rye grass"), near Walla Walla. It became a way station for emigrants, who in 1847 brought a measles infection that flared into an epidemic. Marcus Whitman doctored Cayuse and whites alike, but the Indians had less immunity and died in greater numbers. Believing that Whitman had intentionally saved only the whites, Indians killed both Whitmans and 12 other settlers. The murders set off a war between the Cayuse and the emigrants, which in turn led to the establishment of the Oregon Territory. ♣

An arboreal homestead in one of Puget Sound's utopian colonies. From 1880 to 1890, experiments in socialist idealism flourished around the sound. Photograph by Evadna Cooke, c. 1910. *Washington State Historical Society*

"The Indians are not easily satisfied. .some feel almost to blame us for telling them about eternal realities. One said it was good when they knew nothing but to hunt, eat, drink, and sleep; now it was bad."

An irony-impaired Narcissa Whitman, April 1838

A distinctly Northwestern art first captured national attention in the 1940s and early 50s when a group of artists in Edmonds began creating paintings tinged with Asian spiritualism and imbued with a symbolic sense of landscape. The dean of the Northwest School, as it came to be called, was Mark Tobey, a Wisconsin native who began as a catalog illustrator and society portraitist. A move to Seattle and an encounter with Chinese calligraphy led to Tobey's "white writing" paintings, which vibrate subtly with gray-on-gray lines that convey both the urban pulse and the misty Puget Sound light. Three younger members of the Northwest School—Guy Anderson, Kenneth Callahan, and Morris Graves—grew up near Seattle, where they drew inspiration from the local Asian communities and the rugged yet fog-softened Cascades. In the works of all four

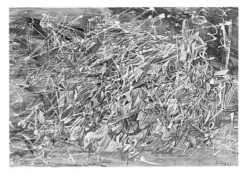

artists, imagery from nature is overlain with a metaphysical language that elevates it from the regional to the universal. ♣

"THE IDEA...IS THE ANCIENT AND, TO ME, FASCINATING ONE of the interrelationship of man, rock and the elements; the creating and disintegration, repeated over and over: man into rock, rock into man, both controlled by sun and elements."

Kenneth Callahan, 1973

Above: Forms Follow Man by Mark Tobey, 1934. The abstract painting represents Tobey's fascination with "white writing." Seattle Art Museum Left: Message by Morris Graves, 1943. Graves often incorporated animals, especially birds, into his work. Seattle Art Museum. Opposite: Northwest Landscape by Kenneth Callahan, 1934. Eugene Fuller Memorial Collection, Seattle Art Museum

Right: Promotional map by Charles S. Fee, produced by the Northern Pacific Railway Company to advertise its route from St. Paul to Seattle, 1896. *Below:* Promotional brochure cover for the Great Northern Railway, 1915. *Both, Washington State Historical Society, Tacoma*

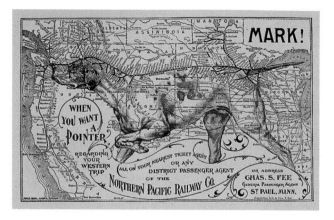

By Land and by Sea

For a dozen years, Washington's sole rail line was a single mule-drawn flatcar on a mile and a half of wooden rails, carrying passengers and freight over the Cascades; in 1863 a steam engine replaced the mules. Throughout the territorial period, small towns laid intersettlement tracks and prayed for a rail connection to the outside world. It finally came in 1883 with the completion of the Northern Pacific Railroad, with Tacoma as its terminus—much to the dismay of Seattle, Bellingham, and other towns that had competed for the honor. The Great Northern Railroad, completed 10 years later, linked Seattle and St. Paul, Minnesota. The railroads made fortunes and opened up the Columbia Basin to farming, although development was restrained until irrigation could bring water to the region.

On the coast, plying the waves was more practical than riding the rails. Washington's ferry system grew in fits and starts to become the largest fleet in the nation and the most important mass-transit system in the state.

"DAKOTA, MONTANA, IDAHO, WASHINGTON AND Oregon wait for this road. It will stimulate all their energies. It will establish vigorous settlements. It will open new regions. It will unfold the hidden treasures of the soil, the mines, the forests, the river, the lakes and the ocean. It will hasten the immigrations by giving confidence to the people that their labors and enterprise shall be rewarded."

George Henry Atkinson, 1878. The Rev Atkinson was a tireless booster for the cause of a Northwest rail line.

Above: A ferry pulls away from the Seattle waterfront. *Photo F. Stuart Westmorland. Left:* Tacoma's Union Station Courthouse, converted from a railroad depot in 1992. Glass sculptor Dale Chihuly created five massive installations for the building in 1994 *Chihuly Studios. Photo Terry Rishel*

Coulee Dam—Looking West by Vanessa Helder, c. 1940. *Cheney Cowles Museum. Opposite above:* Promotional pamphlet for Diablo Dam in the North Cascades, 1929. *Washington State Historical Society, Tacoma*

The Hydropower Age

The awesome might of the Columbia River had long tempted Washingtonians east of the Cascades, who believed that harnessing the river could transform their lives. The idea of a dam began as wild folly on the part of local boosters and culminated in one of the crowning achievements of President Roosevelt's New Deal. When groundbreaking began in 1933, Grand Coulee Dam was touted by FDR's administration as

diablo
HIGHEST IN THE WORLD

the Eighth Wonder of the World; in the words of one reporter, it was "the greatest thing built by the hand of man." The massive project created thousands of jobs and brought irrigation to formerly barren eastern Washington. Almost as an afterthought, it generated vast amounts of hydroelectricity—22,000 megawatts a year, far more than could originally be used by the sparsely populated region. World War II took care of the surplus: Grand Coulee electricity fueled a third of the nation's wartime aluminum output.

Atomic City

Created in utmost secrecy in 1943, the Hanford B nuclear reactor played a leading role in the wartime effort to build an atomic bomb. The site in southeastern Washington was chosen for its isolation; the small local population was bought out and relocated, and some 45,000 workers came in. Plutonium manufactured here was used in the bomb dropped on Nagasaki on August 9, 1945; production continued throughout the Cold War era. The last reactor closed in 1988, and although research continues at Hanford, toxic cleanup of the site is a bigger industry than power generation ever was.

Right: **Publicity photograph of Hanford plutonium worker, c. 1950s.**

World's Fairs

Audacity was not in short supply in 1909, when Washington—then just 20 years into statehood, and still a sparsely populated frontier—held the first of its three world's fairs (more than any other state has held). The Alaska-Yukon-Pacific Exposition celebrated the riches the Klondike Gold Rush had brought to Seattle, while promoting the region's link to what we now call the

Pacific Rim; it helped boost Seattle into prominence over Portland as the Northwest's major metropolis. The 1962 Seattle World's Fair, "Century 21," originally planned to

mark the 50th anniversary of the A-Y-P, spawned a building boom that included several millennial projects: the signature Space Needle and Monorail, as well as the Pacific Science Center designed by Seattle-born architect Minoru Yamasaki. And the environmentally themed 1974 World's Fair Expo in Spokane—the smallest city ever to host a world's fair—sparked the rebirth of that city's riverfront.

Art on the Wall

Toppenish (*TOP-pen-ish*), in south-central Washington, is known as "the mural city." Visitors come here just to see the dozens of murals all around town and to attend Mural-in-a-Day on the first Saturday in June, when more than two dozen artists complete one mural in a single day. Anacortes, on the tip of Fidalgo Island, is adorned with 50 murals, most reproduced from enlarged photographs. Long Beach, on Willapa Bay, has several notable murals, including a delightful scene of oyster harvesters at the turn of the century. West Seattle has 11 historical murals, completed in the 1980s and 1990s, depicting city scenes that range from a steamship landing to an old swimming hole in Lincoln Park.

Toppenish mural celebrating the hops harvest in the Yakima Valley. *Photo Kevin Schafer*

Parks, Wild and Tame

With three national parks, a national monument, and an extensive network of state and city parks, Washington is rich in natural beauty of every conceivable genre, from the neatly groomed to the breathtakingly wild. On the primeval end of the spectrum are North Cascades National Park, most of it inaccessible by vehicle, and Mount St. Helens National Volcanic Monument, created two years after the spectacular 1980 eruption that blew 1,312 feet off the volcano's summit. (Plants and animals are returning to the mountain, despite 21 more eruptions in the 1980s.) Blending wilderness and urban pleasures, Seattle's 535-acre Discovery Park, on the site of a

Above: **Admiralty Head Lighthouse on Whidbey Island.** *Photo Mark Turner. Right:* **Japanese Garden in Tacoma's Point Defiance Park.** Designated by Congress as a military reservation in 1866, 700-acre Point Defiance became a park 20 years later. The Japanese Garden, established in 1965, incorporates giant redwoods and a 1916 pagoda, originally built as a streetcar-line terminus, which may be rented for private events. *Photo F. Stuart Westmorland*

World War II processing center, offers a forest trail, access to Puget Sound beaches, and the best bird-watching opportunities in the city. But for sheer variety of parks and gardens, Spokane may be unsurpassed: it is dotted with 53 neighborhood and community parks, master-planned by the Olmsted brothers (renowned for their design of New York's Central Park), and also boasts more than 1,600 acres of conservation land—all in a city of just 177,000.

Sunset on seastacks, Pacific coast in Olympic National Park. Waves lap at the coast over millennia, eroding the rock and sometimes leaving an isolated pillar called a seastack. *Photo Greg Probst*

Washington's political history is a paradox of enlightened social legislation and tragic racial conflict. Labor organizers found willing converts in Washington's forests and sawmills; by the 1880s they succeeded in reducing the lumber industry workday from 12 to 10 hours, a landmark achievement. Women voted in Territorial Washington during the 1880s and won permanent suffrage in 1910, nine years before national women's suffrage. State-funded public schools, the direct primary vote, and worker's compensation were all enjoyed by Washingtonians by the early 20th century. But other minorities suffered, especially Native Americans—forced by treaty to give up their livelihoods and move to reservations— and Chinese. The latter, who came to work on the railroads and stayed on in low-paying service jobs, were the targets of "Sinophobe" violence in the 1880s. Many were expelled from their homes and businesses. Six decades later, all Japanese-American residents west of the Cascades were sent inland to internment camps for the duration of World War II. ♣

On Strike and on Trial

The year 1919 was a watershed for Washington's labor movement. In February, the Seattle Central Labor Council called a general strike—the first in the nation's history. Sixty thousand workers—one-fifth of the city's population—walked off their jobs for five days, bringing business almost to a standstill. On Armistice Day of the same year, in Centralia, Industrial Workers of the World ("Wobbly") members shot and killed parading American Legionnaires; the slayings resulted in a notorious lynching and gave Washington an enduring reputation for radicalism. The state was 95 percent unionized by the end of World War II, but labor strife continued for decades.

The Four Hour Day

By Hermon F. Titus

4-HOUR DAY

MAY 1 1920

The McNamara Case

A Revolutionary District of the U. M. W. of A.
Principles and Tactics of Revolutionary Socialism

Above: Cover of *The Four Hour Day,* a 1912 pamphlet. Titus was a leader of Seattle's early 20th-century radical movement. *Manuscripts and University Archives, University of Washington Libraries. Opposite above:* A Tacoma labor union pin, 1943. *Opposite below: Seattle, Wash., The Great Depression, Unemployed Battle Police, Winter of 1929–30* by Ronald D. Ginther, 1934. *Both, Washington State Historical Society, Tacoma*

Whole towns shut down

hitching the Coast road, only gypos
Running their beat trucks, no logs on
Gave me rides. Loggers all gone fishing
Chainsaws in a pool of cold oil
On back porches of ten thousand
Split-shake houses, quiet in summer rain.
Hitched north all of Washington
Crossing and re crossing the passes
Blown like dust, no place to work....

Gary Snyder, from "The Late Snow & Lumber Strike
of the Summer of Fifty-Four," 1966

Before the arrival of Europeans, Native dwellings in Washington were among the most unusual in North America. Coastal peoples built cedar "long houses" up to 100 feet long, divided into eight or ten rooms. East of the Cascades, underground pit houses protected their inhabitants from extremes of climate, while nomadic hunting tribes used portable twig-and-pole structures. The first American settlers, mostly unmarried men, made do with crude split-cedar sheds—and some simply moved into hollow tree

Whetting Their Whittles

Surrounded by wood and equipped with pocketknives from a young age, Washington's settlers became adept at whittling and carving practical and fanciful objects. Men in logging camps often re-created scenes of camp life from wood scraps. Other loggers turned to the chainsaw—introduced in the camps in the 1940s—to carve rough-textured sculptures and furniture. Other folk artists created logger genre paintings or logger dolls—the latter sometimes with heads made of dried apples.

The Paulk residence, a contemporary home designed by James Cutler. *Photo Art Grice*
Opposite above: Stump-house on Lindstrom's farm near Edgecomb, 1907. Photograph by Axtells. *Museum of History and Industry, Seattle*
Opposite below: The late Bill Swan of Asotin built a reputation as a leading carver of Western caricatures like this saloon scene, crafted in the 1960s. *Photo Jens Lund*

stumps, many of which were large enough to serve as multiroom homes. Later emigrants from Finland and Sweden re-created the domestic architecture of their Scandinavian homelands, right down to the sharply pitched roofs. Thirteen examples of pioneer cedar structures are on view in Ferndale's Pioneer Park, in the northwestern corner of the state. ♣

Right: Detail of tongue-and-groove construction from a building in Pioneer Park, c. 1870–80. *City of Ferndale Parks and Recreation Department. Photo Michael Sullivan*

Right: The Roeder home, a Craftsman style house in Bellingham. *Whatcom County Parks and Recreation Department.* Below: The Kinnear Mansion, an elaborate Queen Anne Victorian in Seattle. *Museum of History and Industry, Seattle*

Successive booms in logging, mining, railroads, and agriculture created a Washington plutocracy that erected manors in the grand manner. The wealthiest built elaborate estates in a wide range of Victorian styles. Puyallup's founder and first mayor, Ezra Meeker, made (and lost) a fortune growing hops—he was once the richest man in the Pacific Northwest—and his 17-room Italianate Victorian mansion is a prominent landmark in this town of

just 25,000. The Roeder home in Bellingham, built between 1903 and 1908, boasted a state-of-the art vacuum cleaning system and handpainted murals. Today's cyber-barons, the millionaires cloned by Washington's thriving computer industry, are making their own residential statements in a new vernacular, incorporating electronic wizardry into colossal dream homes equipped with every conceivable high-tech gadget. ♣

Interior of the Hauberg residence in Seattle, an award-winning home by the Seattle firm of Olson Sundberg Architects. It was designed to show-case the important art collection of its owners. *Olson Sundberg Architects Photo Michael Jensen*

A hand-tinted lantern slide of the Thornewood garden in Tacoma. Created by the Olmsted brothers between 1908 and 1913, Thornewood enlivened formal English plans with prolific colors and a surprise view of Mount Rainier. *Archive of American Gardens, Smithsonian Institution*

Gardening in Eden

For most of the 19th century, Washingtonians were too pre-occupied with forest-clearing to indulge in gardening as an art; the state's natural state left no one wanting for greenery. Many of Washington's well-known private gardens are thus only a generation or two old, but they compensate in variety and inventiveness. The climate blesses an abundance of plants, both native and introduced, and the dramatic backdrop—mountains, bluffs, rivers, and ocean—invites gardeners to work harmoniously within the landscape. The state flower, the rhododendron, is not surprisingly the focus of many private gardens; lilacs, roses, flowering trees, and conifers are other important elements. Many notable gardens are influenced by an Asian aesthetic: the Bloedel Reserve on Bainbridge Island was designed in part by the Japanese-American landscape designer Fujitaro Kubota, and Washington is a regional center for the cultivation of bonsai, the dwarf trees cherished for centuries by Japanese gardeners.

"THE COOL MOIST CLIMATE OF THE AREA is what makes possible this type of garden, just as a similar climate favors the Luxembourg Gardens of Paris, of which it is so reminiscent...."

James M. Fitch and F. F. Rockwell, commenting on the R. D. Merrill house gardens in Seattle, in Treasury of American Gardens, *1956*

Above: **Ohme Alpine Gardens, Wenatchee. Planted on a rugged hillside, the garden offers dramatic views of the fertile Wenatchee Valley.** *Photo Steve Solum. Left:* **Trestle bridge in the Bloedel Reserve, Bainbridge Island.** *Photo Richard A. Brown*

An Epicure's Delight

They call it simply "the bounty": the native cornucopia that makes Washington one of the worst places in the world in which to attempt an ascetic existence. Abundant seafood, berries, and fruit have always filled Washington's tables. Of late, Seattle has become a culinary mecca: its thriving restaurant scene serves a sophisticated, multinational cuisine grounded in local ingredients prized for their freshness. Other Washington cities aren't far behind. In addition to local crabs, clams, salmon, oysters, and steelhead trout (the state fish), you can sample wild duck, deer, and even bear. The seasonal cherries, pears, and asparagus are

Winery Tours

Sample Washington's vintages, from loganberry liqueur on Whidbey Island to Gewürztraminers and Merlots in the Yakima Valley. Most of Washington's wineries offer tours and tastings. You can plan your itinerary with a map from one of these organizations:

Touring the Washington Wine Country
P.O. Box 61217, Seattle 98121
206-728-2252

Yakima Valley Wine Growers Association
P.O. Box 39, Grandview 98930

Roasted Walla Walla Sweet Onions

The original Walla Walla onion seeds came from Corsica

    4 medium Walla Walla sweet onions, peeled
    1 tbsp. olive oil
    ½ cup + 2 tbsp. toasted pine nuts
    3 oz. unsalted butter, softened
    ½ tsp. lemon zest
    ½ tsp. chopped fresh rosemary
    Salt and black pepper
    ⅓ cup grated Parmesan cheese

Preheat oven to 375° and fire up an outdoor grill. Cut onions in half, top to bottom. Brush with oil and grill cut side down until grill marks form. Finish cooking in oven until tender, about 25 minutes. Make pine nut butter: pulse ½ cup nuts fine in food processor. Add butter, zest, and seasonings. Process well. Spread tender onions with nut butter. Return to oven and cook just until butter is melted, about 2 minutes. Sprinkle with grated cheese and whole nuts; garnish with lemon wedges and rosemary sprigs.

Tom Douglas, the Dahlia Lounge, Seattle

among the most delectable anywhere, and the liquid accompaniments are equally impressive. Washington's wineries are internationally acclaimed, and the state's breweries nearly as celebrated—from the venerable Rainier and Olympia brands to many lesser-known, high-quality microbrews. And there's good reason to believe the nation's current coffee craze started here, with Seattle-based (and now nearly ubiquitous) Starbucks.

Above: Starbucks labels. *Starbucks Coffee Company. Right:* Olympia Brewing Company label, c. 1915. *Private collection*

Opposite: "High Stall" at the Pike Place Farmer's Market in Seattle's Historical District. *Photo Joel W. Rogers/Off Shoot Stock*

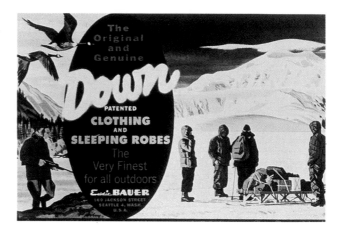

Up and Away

With tall peaks dominating the view, it stands to reason that recreation in Washington has always had an upward angle. Ignoring the warnings of Native guides, who believed the mountain was inhabited by an evil spirit, Hazard Stevens became the first to reach the summit of Mount Rainier in 1870. Mount Baker had been conquered two years earlier, on a 10-day ascent in which the party subsisted solely on bacon, bread, and tea. Washington's peaks have since been a training ground for American mountaineers who went on to lofty feats in the Himalaya and other international ranges; Seattle's Jim Whittaker became the first American to reach the top of Everest in a 1963 expedition.

Washington native Eddie Bauer invented the down jacket in the 1930s, and Seattle-based retailer Recreational Equipment Inc. (REI) leads the way in outfitting outdoorsfolk with the latest in crampons, backpacks, and freeze-dried dinners. Other local innovations have opened the high country to even more people: the Baby Jogger, invented in Yakima in 1983, lets active parents take their offspring into the fast lane. And the Seattle Foot—a high-tech prosthesis introduced by the University of Washington in 1985—enables lower-limb amputees to walk, run, ski, rock climb, and hike.

"Climbing over a rocky ridge...

we found ourselves within a circular crater...filled with a solid bed of snow.... Van Tramp detected the odor of sulphur... jets of steam and smoke were observed issuing from the crevices of the rocks which formed the rim on the northern side. Never was a discovery more welcome! Hastening forward, we both exclaimed, as we warmed our chilled and benumbed extremities over one of Pluto's fires, that here we would pass the night, secure against freezing to death, at least."

Hazard Stevens's account of his pioneering 1870 ascent of Mount Rainier, Atlantic Monthly, *1876*

Rock climber in breathtaking suspension on Eagle's Nest in Lyle, Washington. *Photo Eric Sanford/Weststock*

On the Water

Whether kayaking the bays, rafting the rivers, or sailing the coast, Washingtonians are avid aquatic enthusiasts. The hydroplane was invented here in 1929, and is honored by big hydroplane races every summer at Seattle's Seafair festival. Other native inventions include water skis, introduced in 1928 by a young Seattleite named Don Ibsen, and the Pocock shell, the standard-bearer of competitive rowing. The upscale Seattle suburb of Bellevue is a yachting mecca, counting among its residents some University of Washington alumni who sail across Lake Washington to football games at the campus. Cruising through the San Juans is another favorite pastime of sailors, and

Above: Sailboat racing on Seattle's Lake Union, in the heart of the city. *Photo Gail Mooney Right:* Seattle waterski enthusiasts pose with their gear for an early 1940s photo. *Museum of History and Industry, Seattle*

the Columbia Gorge is one of the prime windsurfing venues in the world. Pioneering Washington recently became one of the first places to restrict noisy jet skis—good news for boaters and others who prefer to recreate in tranquility.

Sea kayakers approaching Strawberry Island on Rosario Strait, northern Puget Sound. *Photo Joel W. Rogers*

"These movements are almost impossible

to put on paper or explain by word of mouth; they have to be demonstrated by constant practice until the oarsman gets the true 'feel' of the boat."

George Yeoman Pocock, developer of the Pocock rowing shell, 1972

Above: Movie art for Frank Herbert's *Dune* (1965), a science fiction classic. *Ron Borst/Hollywood Movie Posters Right:* Cover of the first issue of *Poetry Northwest* magazine, June 1959. *Poetry Northwest. Opposite above:* Mary McCarthy, born in 1912. *Photo Thomas Victor. Courtesy Harriet Spurlin*

Literature "By and By"

In 1889, local historian Edmond Meany sighed, "There is no time [in Washington] to devote to the production or the appreciation of a distinctive literature.... Literature will be fostered by and by." As late as 1947, when the poet Theodore Roethke arrived in Seattle to teach at the University of Washington, the English department chairman told him, "You're the only serious practicing poet within 1,500 miles." Some native writers, such as Mary McCarthy, found their niche only after leaving their home state. Yet by the 1960s Washington had developed a vigorous and distinctive literature, thanks in large part to Roethke and his illustrious students—among them Richard Hugo, Carolyn Kizer, and Richard Wright. *Poetry Northwest,* founded by Kizer and published in Washington since 1959, is the oldest U.S. magazine devoted to poetry. But poetry is just part of the story: Washington's diverse chorus of voices embraces Tom Robbins's quirky lyricism, Frank Herbert's sci-fi epics, David Guterson's thoughtful historical novels, Richard White's "new Western history," Raymond Carver's minimalist stories, and the novels and screenplays of Sherman Alexie, a young Spokane–Coeur d'Alene Indian.

POETRY NORTHWEST
JUNE, 1959
NUMBER 1

"NAMES, OFTEN, WERE FREAKISH IN THE PACIFIC Northwest, particularly girls' names. In the Episcopal boarding school I went to later, in Tacoma, there was a girl called De Vere Utter, and there was a girl called Rocena and another called Hermoine....You do not hear names like those often, in any case, east of the Cascade Mountains; they belong to the frontier, where books and libraries were few and memory seems to have been oral, as in the time of Homer."

Mary McCarthy, Memories of
a Catholic Girlhood, *1957*

"Rain fell on Skagit Valley.

It fell in sweeps and it fell in drones. It fell in unending cascades of cheap Zen jewelry. It fell on the dikes. It fell on the firs. It fell on the downcast necks of the mallards.

And it rained a screaming. And it rained a rawness. And it rained a plasma. And it rained a disorder."

Tom Robbins, Another Roadside Attraction, *1971*

Tom Robbins in his hometown of La Conner, Washington, 1977. Robbins's best-known novel, *Another Roadside Attraction*, is a playful fable of eccentric rural Washingtonians. *Photo AP/Wide World Photos*

Washington on Stage and Screen

The state's first recorded theatrical performance—a recitation in the dining room of Olympia's one hotel, admission 25 cents—took place in 1853. By the turn of the century, there were theaters all over the state, many of them grand terra-cotta edifices like the Auditorium in Spokane (which was for decades the finest theater building in the West), Squire's Opera House in Seattle, and the Gaiety in Walla Walla. Greek immigrant Alexander Pantages opened his first Seattle movie house in 1902; by 1920, his theater circuit was the strongest in America.

Above: Wallace Beery and Marie Dressler in a still from *Tugboat Annie* (1933). *Photofest. Right:* Seattle's 5th Avenue Theatre, a movie palace built in 1926, is now home to a musical theater company. *Photo Dick Busher. Opposite above:* Tom Hanks lost in a dream in Pike Place Market, from *Sleepless in Seattle* (1993). *Opposite below:* Kelsey Grammer in the title role of TV's *Frasier,* which premiered in 1993. *Both, Photofest*

Today theater and film thrive at the Washington Shakespeare Festival in Olympia, at Seattle's International Film Festival, and in many small drama companies throughout the state. And Washington itself

has played a role in movies from 1933's *Tugboat Annie* to the 1998 indie hit *Smoke Signals,* based on a Sherman Alexie screenplay about young Native Americans. In addition, three television series—*Northern Exposure, Twin Peaks,* and *Frasier*—were shot or set in Washington.

Reel-Life Washington

Tugboat Annie Inspired by true story of Tacoma ferry operator

The Egg and I Fred MacMurray and Claudette Colbert in 1947 adaptation of Betty MacDonald's memoir—first appearance of Ma and Pa Kettle

It Happened at the World's Fair Elvis at the Space Needle! 1963

Cinderella Liberty Jack Nicholson as a sailor in shabby Seattle; 1973

McQ John Wayne as a cop living on a boat in Fremont; 1974

The Parallax View Warren Beatty thriller

An Officer and a Gentleman Modern-day romance with Deborah Winger and Richard Gere; 1982

Frances Jessica Lange as Seattle native Frances Farmer; 1983

Trouble in Mind Alan Rudolph film featuring old Seattle Art Museum transformed into a gangster's mansion; 1985

Harry and the Hendersons Sasquatch fantasy starring John Lithgow; 1987

The Fabulous Baker Boys Michelle Pfeiffer and the Bridges brothers

Singles Bridget Fonda and Matt Dillon with grunge backdrop; 1992

Sleepless in Seattle Tom Hanks/Meg Ryan romance; 1993

Movers and Players

For its modest size (population about 520,000), Seattle is
unusually well endowed with music and dance resources. It
is one of only six cities in the nation with a major symphony,
opera, and ballet company. The Seattle Symphony Orchestra,
established in 1903, is the oldest major cultural institution in
the Pacific Northwest and the region's largest employer of
artists. In the autumn of 1998, it moved into a new home
befitting its stature: Benaroya Hall, designed by local architects Loschky Marquardt & Neesholm and graced with important art works by Robert Rauschenberg, Dale Chihuly, and
others. Since the 1970s, the Seattle Opera has been world-

renowned for its Wagner productions, notably the Ring Cycle. Seattle was also the home of William Bergsma (1921–1994), important both as director of the University of Washington School of Music and as a composer of opera (*The Wife of Martin Guerre*), orchestral works, and ballet suites. On the dance scene, Washington claims three pioneering choreographers—Merce Cunningham, Robert Joffrey, and Mark Morris—and the Pacific Northwest Ballet tours nationally from its Seattle base. (Famed children's book author Maurice Sendak designed the sets for the company's *Nutcracker Suite.*)

Washington also supports thriving folk music and jazz scenes. The electric guitar is said to have been invented in Washington by Paul Tutmarc in 1931, a claim disputed by Les Paul and others. Rock icon Jimi Hendrix, a native, will soon be honored with a Seattle museum of his memorabilia, and in the 1980s Seattle was the epicenter of the grunge-rock phenomenon, epitomized by the bands Nirvana and Pearl Jam.

Above: A Pacific Northwest Ballet performance of Tchaikovsky's *Nutcracker Suite. Photo Joel W. Rogers. Left:* Choreographer Mark Morris performing in *Rondo.* Now based in New York, Morris has boldly bridged dance, film, opera, and choral works. *Photo Julie Lemberger/ StageImage*

Right: Host of Listeners by Robert Helm, 1997. Helm, whose family came to the Palouse region of Washington in the late 19th century, began as a sculptor but now renders his compositions in paint. *Myerson & Nowinski Art Associates Below: Obos I* by George Tsutakawa, 1956. Tsutakawa's sculpture is the first in a series named after Tibetan shrines. *Seattle Art Museum*

Influenced by native traditions and Asian aesthetics, by local environment and global perspectives, Washington's vibrant contemporary art scene transcends regionalism. Outdoor, site-specific sculpture is an important theme —not surprisingly, in a state that treasures its open-air splendors. Seattle native George Tsutakawa (1910–1987) gained international renown for his public fountains in North America and Japan, as well as for enigmatic stone sculptures inspired by Himalayan pilgrim shrines. Marvin Oliver's monumental works in cedar, bronze, cast glass, and enameled steel—totem poles and stylized whale fins—bring together ancient forms and modern

materials. There's a playful streak here, too, seen in Richard Beyer's *People Waiting for the Interurban* in Seattle's Fremont neighborhood—a life-size group of commuters (and dog) that are frequently "dressed" by passers-by—and in Jack Mackie's *Dancer's Series Steps on Broadway*, bronze footsteps accompanied by dance instructions. Buster Simpson's environmental artworks and Richard Haag's landscape architecture represent conceptual and pragmatic ends of the earthworks spectrum.

Boats in the Harbor by Sumio Arima, 1923. Born in Tokyo in 1901, Arima came to Seattle as a teenager and eventually became the publisher of his father's Japanese- and English-language newspaper. *Reproduced with permission of Wing Luke Asian Museum Photo Paul Macapia*

Right: Sculptor Richard Beyer's playful *People Waiting for the Interurban,* 1978, a cast-aluminum tableau in Seattle's Fremont neighborhood. Beyer's other public sculptures include *Sasquatch* at Pike Place Market and *Kingstones* in front of the KING-TV studios. *Photo Kurt Smith/Seattle Post-Intelligencer. Below: Milltown Exit* by Fay Jones, 1984. *Seattle Art Museum*

Many of Washington's most important artists produce work that defies regional stereotyping. Jacob Lawrence, who moved to Seattle in 1971 to teach art at the University of Washington, draws on the Harlem of his youth in paintings such as his 60-panel series, *The Migration of the Negro.* Michael Spafford's *Twelve Labors of Hercules,* commissioned for the Washington State Capitol and now part of the Microsoft Art Collection, simplifies and reinterprets the Greek myth. And video artist Gary Hill experiments with strobe-lit installations that suggest the elusive images in Plato's cave. ♣

The Studio by Jacob Lawrence, 1977. Lawrence has said that his vivid palette was inspired by his childhood in Depression-era Harlem. "Our homes were very decorative, full of a lot of pattern and color. Because we were so poor, the people used this as a means of brightening their lives." After his 1985 retirement from teaching art at the University of Washington, Lawrence continued to lecture in art history seminars and studio art classes. *Seattle Art Museum. Below: Apple Picker God by Tim Fowler, 1995. Garde-Rail Gallery, Seattle*

"I LIKE TOOLS. I LIKE TO WORK WITH THEM, AND I LIKE to look at them....In many of the religious panels of the Renaissance, you see the same tools as carpenters use today....[T]hey've become a symbol of order and meaning to me." *Jacob Lawrence, interview in Art News, 1984*

NATIVE EXPRESSIONS

Washington has attracted Indian artists from diverse tribes and regions, many of whom integrate ancestral elements with contemporary materials and subjects. Superb traditional masks and totems are still being created, but so are less conventional glasswork, large-scale sculpture, and mixed-media pieces. Perhaps the most eminent example of this fusion was James Schoppert, the subject of a 1998 exhibit at Seattle's Burke Museum that also traveled to the Smithsonian. Schoppert, who died in 1992 at age 45, was a sculptor, painter, poet, and spokesman

for the Native arts. Born in Alaska to Tlingit and German parents, he received a classical art education while studying the spiritual origins of Native art. His cedar and poplar panels were carved with traditional designs using handmade knives, but painted in a bright, expressionistic palette. ♣

Above: Elk Spirit, glass sculpture by Caroline Orr (Colville Confederate Tribes), 1994. Courtesy the artist. Left: Facing You, glass and steel sculpture by Marvin Oliver (Quinault/Isleta Pueblo), 1997. Private collection. Photo courtesy the artist

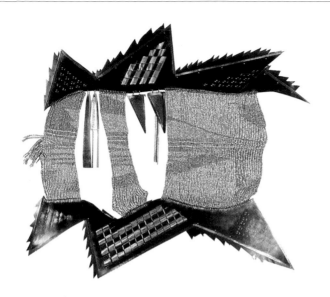

Left: Star Burst by Gail Tremblay, 1990. Born in Buffalo, New York, of Onandaga/Micmac and French Canadian ancestry, Tremblay lives and teaches in Olympia. In addition to her work in the visual arts, she is a prolific poet, singer, and songwriter. *Courtesy the artist. Below: Stillwater,* carved and polychromed cedar sculpture by James G. Schoppert (Tlingit), 1983. *Washington State Arts Commission/Skagit Valley College. Photo courtesy Donette Lee*

Maybe it's the crystalline glaciers or the volcanic lava—clearly, something in the Washington landscape inspires glass artists to push the limits of their fragile, supple medium. Foremost among them is Dale Chihuly, whose Pilchuck Glass School in Stanwood has become an internationally acclaimed art-glass center. Born in Tacoma in 1941, Chihuly has created some

Above: Celestial Dream Persian Set with Red Ruby Lip Wraps by Dale Chihuly, 1997. Photo Theresa Batty. Left: Icicle Creek Chandelier by Dale Chihuly, 1997. This 10-foot-high sculpture—located at the Sleeping Lady Retreat Center outside of Leavenworth—is Chihuly's only permanent outdoor installation. John Marshall Outdoor Photography. Both, Chihuly Studios

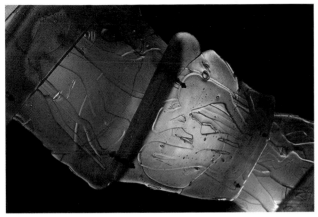

of the largest installations of hand-blown glass, including *Puget Sound Forms* for the Seattle Aquarium and five massive installations for Tacoma's Union Station Courthouse. His *Macchia* series, begun in 1981, uses up to 300 colors in each glass form; his first permanent outdoor installation, *Icicle Creek Chandelier,* was created in 1996 for a conference center in Leavenworth. Chihuly's achievements are even more remarkable considering that he lost the sight in his left eye in a 1976 auto accident. ▲

Celtic Echoes

Lawyer, businessman, millionaire, and diplomat Sam Hill tried to establish a Quaker agricultural community on 7,000 acres overlooking the Columbia River, in Klickitat County. That dream failed, but his full-sized replica of Stonehenge—unravaged by time—still stands as a memorial to the dead of World War I. Begun in 1918 and finished in 1930, the mammoth monument is made of reinforced concrete, molded in forms lined with crumpled tin to create a distressed texture.

Market Value

Opened in 1907, Seattle's Pike Place Market is the oldest continuously operating farmers' market in the United States. It began as an outlet for farmers throughout the region; per-

manent buildings were erected in 1917. Threatened by urban renewal in the 1960s, the open-air market was saved by a grassroots movement led by local architect Victor Steinbrueck. Today it comprises more than 200 small businesses selling everything from live lobsters to baby lettuce to silver jewelry.

Bing's Things

The Bing Crosby Collection at Gonzaga University in Spokane memorializes the college's most famous alumnus, Harry Louis (Bing) Crosby (1903–1977). Here you'll find records, photographs, and trophies from the collection of the late crooner, whose road to Hollywood, Rio, and elsewhere began in Walla Walla.

Seattle/Washington

In the plaza of Seattle's Washington State Convention and Trade Center stands an apt and unusual 28-foot twin portrait. Twenty-four aluminum profiles of Native leader Chief Seattle form a framework for English ivy; a template of George Washington's profile acts as a wind vane that trims the ivy as it revolves. Artist Buster Simpson aligned *Seattle George* with true north and had Chief Seattle's famous 1855 speech sandblasted in the walkway. "Eventually, as the vines cover the head, Chief Seattle will become a memory," says Simpson.

A Really Long Island

Nearly 50 miles from stem to stern, Whidbey Island in northern Puget Sound is the longest island in the continental United States. New York lost the contest by congressional decision: its Long Island is technically a peninsula.

Past Petrified

Gingko Petrified Forest State Park, just outside the town of Vantage, is the only place in the world you'll find petrified specimens of the prehistoric gingko trees that thrived here some 15 million years ago, when the climate was tropical. Molten lava buried the forests; the most recent ice age exposed them. A stop at the park's visitor center provides an outstanding view of the Columbia River and basalt cliffs.

Great People

A selective listing of native Washingtonians, concentrating on the arts.

Judy Collins (b. 1939), singer and songwriter

Brock Adams (b. 1927), congressman (1965–77), senator (1987–92), U.S. secretary of transportation

Bob Barker (b. 1923), host of daytime TV shows; beauty pageant emcee

Lynda Barry (b. 1956), cartoonist

Chester Carlson (1906–1968), inventor of the photocopier machine, founder of the company that became Xerox Corp.

Carol Channing (b. 1923), actress and singer

Dale Chihuly (b. 1941), glass artist

Chuck Close (b. 1940), painter

Bing Crosby (1903–1977), singer and actor, won 1944 Academy Award for *Going My Way*

Merce Cunningham (b. 1919), modern dancer and choreographer

William O. Douglas (1898–1980), associate justice of U.S. Supreme Court 1939–75 (longest term in history)

John Elway (b. 1960), Denver Broncos quarterback; led team to three Super Bowls

Bill Gates (b. 1955), co-founder of Microsoft Corporation

Jimi Hendrix (1942–1970), musician

Henry "Scoop" Jackson (1912–1983), U.S. representative and senator, ran for president in 1972 and 1976

Robert Joffrey (1930–1988), modern-dance choreographer, founder of Joffrey Ballet

Kamiakin (1800–1880), Yakima Indian chief, led his people during Indian wars of 1855

Hank Ketcham (b. 1920), cartoonist, "Dennis the Menace"

Gary Larson (b. 1950), cartoonist, "The Far Side"

Phil Mahre (b. 1957), alpine skier; won silver medal in slalom, 1980 Olympic Winter Games; first American to win gold medal in men's skiing (slalom, 1984)

Mary McCarthy (1912–1989), novelist, essayist, and short-story writer

Mark Morris (b. 1956), modern dancer and choreographer

Dixy Lee Ray (1914–1994), first woman governor in Washington history

Jimmy Rodgers (b. 1933), musician ("Honeycomb," "Kisses Sweeter Than Wine")

Theodore Roethke (1908–1963), poet, won 1954 Pulitzer Prize

Seathl (1786–1866), chief of several Puget Sound peoples; city of Seattle is named for him

Alice B. Toklas (1877–1967), cook, author, and companion of Gertrude Stein

. . . and Great Places

Some interesting derivations of Washington place names.

Aberdeen   At the junction of the Chehalis and Wishkah rivers, Aberdeen is, like its Scottish namesake, a fishing town. The Gaelic word means "the meeting of two rivers."

Anacortes   Named in 1876 by town planner Amos Bowman, who "Hispanicized" his wife's name, Anna Curtis.

Bonneville   Honors Gen. Benjamin Louis Eulalie de Bonneville, French-born U.S. Army hero of the Mexican War.

Bush Prairie   For George Bush, who in 1845 was the first African American to settle in what is now Washington State.

Cape Flattery   Named by England's Capt. James Cook, who thought he saw a harbor at the southern entrance of the Juan de Fuca Strait; closer examination proved him wrong.

Cashmere   Picturesque town named for India's Kashmir Valley.

Chelan   City, lake, river, falls, butte, and mountains take their name from the native *Tsill-ane,* "deep water."

Cle Elum   From the Indian word meaning "swift water."

Columbia   The river is named for the ship *Columbia Rediviva,* whose American captain, Robert Gray, discovered it in 1792.

Dosewallips River   Derived from Dos-wail-opsh, a legendary man in Twana Indian mythology. He was turned into a mountain that is the river's source.

Friday Harbor   Named after Friday, a Hawaiian man brought to the island by the Hudson's Bay Company to tend its sheep.

Humptulips   From an Indian term meaning "chilly region."

Juan de Fuca   The strait is named for its alleged discoverer, Juan de Fuca, whose 16th-century exploits may have been largely or wholly invented.

Klickitat   From the Chinook term meaning "beyond."

La Conner   Named by the owner of an 1860s trading post for his wife, L(ouise) A(nne) Conner.

Pilchuck   From Chinook jargon words meaning "red water," describing the color of the creek.

Puyallup   *("Pew-ALLOP")* The name of the local Indian tribe; means "generous people."

Snoqualmie   Two towns, a river, falls, and pass, are named after the area's natives, whose tribal name meant "moon."

Toppenish   Yakima for "sloping and spreading land."

Walla Walla   Derived from a Nez Perce and Cayuse word, *walatsa,* "running water."

Nisqually   French explorers called the local natives *nez quarre,* meaning "square nose."

WASHINGTON BY THE SEASONS
A Perennial Calendar of Events and Festivals

Here is a selective listing of events that take place each year in the months noted; we suggest calling ahead to local chambers of commerce for dates and details.

January

Grayland
Penguin Plunge
"Polar bears" from around the world brave the frigid Pacific.

Leavenworth
Great Bavarian Ice Fest
Snow-sculpting, dogsled contests, and sleigh rides.

Winthrop
International Snowshoe Softball Tournament
Same rules, different footwear.

February

Forks
Art on the Hill
Featuring works by Olympic Peninsula artists.

Seattle
Fat Tuesday
The state's Mardi Gras; lots of music, Spam-carving contest.

Seattle
Festival Sundiata
Northwest's largest celebration of African-American culture.

Tacoma
Wintergrass
Bluegrass festival.

Toppenish
Cowboy Poetry Gathering

March

Ocean Shore
Beachcombers Fun Fair
Beachcombed treasures, marine science, crafts, food.

Othello
Sandhill Crane Festival
Bus tours, guided hikes to view migrating cranes.

Tenino
Old-Time Music Festival
Three big shows with fiddles, guitars, accordions, banjos.

April

Forks
Rainfest
Arts festival in town that gets 10–12 feet of rain annually.

Mt. Vernon
Skagit Valley Tulip Festival
Runs two weeks in the nation's top tulip-growing region.

Port Orchard
Seagull Calling Contest
Competitions for best costume and seagull call.

Port Townsend
Rhododendron Festival

Seattle
Cherry Blossom and Japanese Cultural Festival

Tacoma
Daffodil Festival

Wenatchee
State Apple Blossom Festival
Apple capital celebrates with parades, craft show, and the crowning of the Apple Queen.

May

Leavenworth
Mai Fest
A parade and plenty of "oom-pah" music celebrate the town's Bavarian roots.

Seattle
International Film Festival
150 films from around the world; through June.

Seattle
Northwest Folklife Festival
More than 5,000 folk performers and artists.

Sequim
Irrigation Festival
The wonders of irrigation celebrated with a parade, picnic, flower show, and art displays.

Spokane
Lilac Festival

June

Blaine
Hands Across the Border Peace Arch Celebration

Bellingham
Lummi Stommish Festival
Event on the Lummi Reserve stems from the potlatch; war canoe races, salmon bake, traditional dances, and more.

Toppenish
Mural-in-a-Day Festival

July

Bainbridge Island
Bainbridge in Bloom
Garden tours.

Port Angeles
Juan de Fuca Festival
Workshops, music, art, food, and kids' activities.

Seattle
Seafair
Seattle's biggest summer festival; jet boat races, torchlight parade, airshow, and carnival.

Seattle
The Bite
Sample the offerings of top regional chefs, breweries.

August

Leavenworth
International Accordion Celebration
Competitions and workshops.

Long Beach
International Kite Festival
Billed as the largest kite festival in the western hemisphere.

Neah Bay
Makah Days
Canoe races, Indian dances, Native arts, a salmon bake, and fireworks.

Suquamish
Chief Seattle Days
Near Seattle's gravesite; includes canoe races, dancing, art show.

September

Ellensburg
Rodeo
Among the top 10 U.S. rodeos, it runs over Labor Day weekend.

Odessa
Deutschesfest
Hosted by the local German community.

Pullman
National Lentil Festival
Sample lentil lasagna and lentil ice cream.

Seattle
Bumbershoot
City's biggest arts festival, held Labor Day weekend, includes theater and music events.

Yakima
Central Washington State Fair
One of the Northwest's best agricultural exhibitions.

October

Bellevue
Japan Week

Leavenworth
Wenatchee River Salmon Festival
The salmon's return is honored.

Long Beach
Water Music Festival
A wide variety of chamber music.

Port Townsend
Kinetic Sculpture Race

Imaginative vehicles test their mettle on land, mud, and water.

Shelton
Oysterfest
Wine tasting, oyster shucking, and free entertainment.

November

Leavenworth
Christkindlmarkt
Emulates the great German Christmas markets.

Roslyn
Winterfest
Community lighting, caroling, sleigh rides in the hometown of TV's *Northern Exposure*.

Yakima
Thanksgiving in Wine Country
Taste premium wines and food.

December

Seattle
Christmas Ship Festival

Sunnyside
Country Christmas Lighted Farm Implement Parade
Illuminated combines, threshers, and tractors honor the Yakima Valley's agricultural heritage.

Wapato
Longhouse Christmas Celebration and Pow Wow
Native American performers.

Whidbey Island
Winter on Whidbey
Wine tasting, caroling, bell choirs, and ice skating.

WHERE TO GO
Museums, Attractions, Gardens, and Other Arts Resources

Call for seasons and hours when open.

Museums

AMERICAN HOP MUSEUM
22 So. B St., Toppenish, 509-865-4677
In restored Hop Growers Supply building; focuses on Yakima Valley hop crop from 1805 to present.

BELLEVUE ART MUSEUM
301 Bellevue Square, Bellevue, 206-454-3322
Contemporary American, decorative, and regional art and traveling shows. A new facility is planned to open around the year 2000.

BURKE MUSEUM OF NATURAL HISTORY
AND CULTURE
University of Washington campus, Seattle, 206-543-5590
Depicts evolution of Washington's land and people over 500 million years.

CHENEY COWLES MEMORIAL MUSEUM
2316 W. 1st Ave., Spokane, 509-456-3931
Indian artifacts and exhibits on the history of the Inland Empire. Next door is Campbell House, a restored early-20th-century mansion.

COAST GUARD MUSEUM NORTHWEST
Pier 36 at 1519 Alaskan Way S., Seattle, 206-217-6993
One of only two U.S. Coast Guard museums; eclectic exhibits include a piece of HMS *Bounty's* rudder, 1850s lighthouse clock.

COLUMBIA RIVER EXHIBITION OF HISTORY,
SCIENCE, AND TECHNOLOGY
95 Lee Blvd., Richland, 509-943-9000
Displays, interactive exhibits, and videos on the Hanford Nuclear Reservation, nuclear power in general.

FRYE ART MUSEUM
704 Terry Ave., Seattle, 206-622-9250
Collections of 19th- and 20th-century European and American paintings, important works from the Munich Secession.

HENRY ART GALLERY
University of Washington campus, Seattle, 206-543-2280
Washington's oldest art gallery houses 19th- and 20th-century landscape paintings; photography and prints; contemporary Japanese works; textiles.

LEWIS COUNTY HISTORICAL MUSEUM
599 NW Front St., Centralia, 360-748-0831
Showcases local Chehalis tribe artifacts, and a major exhibit on labor history.

MAKAH MUSEUM
East end of Neah Bay, off Hwy 112, 360-645-2711
One of the best U.S. Native American museums, emphasizes artifacts from Ozette site; fine displays of ancient Makah life.

MARYHILL MUSEUM OF ART
SR 14, 2.7 miles west of U.S. 97, 509-773-3733
Flemish-style chateau was home to eccentric millionaire Sam Hill; houses Rodin sculpture, Native basketry, Russian icons. Open mid-March through mid-November.

MUSEUM OF FLIGHT
9404 E. Marginal Way S., Seattle, 206-764-5720
Near Boeing's private airport, its dramatic steel-and-glass gallery is hung with dozens of planes. Schoolkids "launch" the space shuttle at Challenger Learning Center. Don't miss the "Aerocar."

MUSEUM OF NORTHWEST ART
121 S. 1st St., La Conner, 360 466 4446
Paintings, glass, and sculpture by regional artists, some from the Northwest School.

SEATTLE ART MUSEUM
100 University St., Seattle, 206-654-3100
World-class collections of Asian, African, and North-west Coast Indian art; year-round traveling exhibits.

SEATTLE ASIAN ART MUSEUM
Volunteer Park, Seattle, 206-654-3100
One of the best and largest Asian art collections in the U.S.; six galleries devoted to Japanese art.

TACOMA ART MUSEUM
1123 Pacific Ave., Tacoma, 253-272-4258
Permanent exhibits of Dale Chihuly glass sculptures, plus works by 19th- and 20th-century American artists and the Sara Little Center for Design Research.

WASHINGTON STATE HISTORY MUSEUM
1911 Pacific Ave., Tacoma, 253-272-3500
Interactive exhibits include a Salish cedar plank house, reconstructed frontier store, simulated Boeing B-17 flight, and a video trip down the Columbia.

WESTERN WASHINGTON UNIVERSITY OUTDOOR SCULPTURE COLLECTION
Western Washington University, Bellingham, 360-650-3963
Works by regional, national, and international artists from 1960 to the present.

WHALE MUSEUM
62 1st St. N., Friday Harbor, San Juan Island, 800 562 8832
Whale and porpoise displays, a whale mural, whale songs, and an interactive video about snoring whales.

WHATCOM MUSEUM OF HISTORY AND ART
121 Prospect St., Bellingham, 360-676-6981
The state's second-largest museum, in former city hall. Regional history, contemporary art, and period tools, toys, and clothing; extensive Northwest Indian art.

WING LUKE MEMORIAL MUSEUM
414 8th St. S., Seattle, 206-623-5124
Changing exhibits of Asian folk art.

WORLD KITE MUSEUM AND HALL OF FAME
104 Pacific Hwy N., Long Beach, 360-642-4020
Fascinating displays of artistic, scientific, and com-mercial kites in a city known for its annual kite festival.

YAKAMA INDIAN NATIONAL CULTURAL CENTER
0.5 mi. north of Toppenish on US 97, 509-865-2800
Chronicles the Yakama (Yakima) Indians' history, with a 76-foot-high winter lodge, research library, theater, and dioramas.

Attractions

BOEING PRODUCTION FACILITY
Off I-5 exit 189, then 3.5 miles west on SR 526, Everett, 425-544-1264
Eleven-story assembly plant has the largest volume of any building in the world. Free 90-minute tours.

CENTER FOR WOODEN BOATS
1010 Valley St., Seattle, 206-382-2628
Antique wooden canoes; all kinds of pleasure craft and workboats; classes and workshops. Next door at Northwest Seaport is three-masted schooner *Wawona*.

FORT VANCOUVER
E. Evergreen Blvd., I-5 exit 1C at Mill Plain Blvd., Vancouver, 360-696-7655
The state's oldest city, now a national historic site; Officers' Row—21 elegant turn-of-the-century homes—is the only fully restored example in the U.S.

GRAND COULEE DAM

Coulee Dam, 509-633-9265

Free tours of one of the world's most massive concrete structures, completed in 1941 to harness the Columbia River for electrical power and irrigation.

HANFORD SCIENCE CENTER

825 Jadwin Ave., Richland, 509-376-6374

Tells the story of the Hanford nuclear facility, site of the world's first plutonium production plants.

KLONDIKE GOLD RUSH NATIONAL HISTORIC PARK

117 S. Main St., Seattle, 206-553-7220

This indoor "park" commemorates Seattle's role in the 1897 gold rush with mining relics, clothing, and audiovisual programs.

WASHINGTON STATE CAPITOL

14th Ave. and Capitol Way, Olympia, 360-586-8687

Capitol building's 287-foot dome is one of the world's largest; rotunda has a Tiffany chandelier. Nearby are the 1908 governor's mansion and conservatory.

Homes and Gardens

BELLEVUE BOTANICAL GARDEN

12001 Main St., Wilburton Hill Park, Bellevue, 425-452-2749

Demonstration gardens featuring Northwest native plants, plus 36 acres of native habitats.

BLOEDEL RESERVE

7571 N.E. Dolphin Dr., Bainbridge Island, 206-842-7631

Once a private estate, 150 acres feature formal and Japanese gardens, bird marsh, and woodlands.

HULDA KLAGER LILAC GARDENS

115 S. Pekin, Woodland, 206-225-8996

Over 500 lilac bushes, many hybridized by Mrs. Klager between 1903 and 1960.

LAKEWOLD GARDENS

12317 Gravelly Lake Dr., Tacoma, 206-584-4106

Ten acres of rare plants and a large collection of rhododendrons and Japanese maples.

MANITO PARK

Grand Blvd. between 17th and 25th Aves., Spokane, 509-625-6622

Beautiful lilacs—Spokane is the "Lilac City"—and a Japanese garden grace this 90-acre park.

MEEKER MANSION

312 Spring St., Puyallup, 253-848-1770

This Italianate Victorian was home to Puyallup's first mayor, Ezra Meeker.

MEERKERK RHODODENDRON GARDENS

On Resort Rd. 1.5 mi. south and 0.2 mi. east of Greenbank, 360-678-1912

Ten acres of rhododendrons within a 53-acre woodland reach peak bloom late April to early May.

OHME GARDENS

3327 Ohme Rd., Wenatchee, 509-662-5785

See page 65.

PACIFIC RIM BONSAI COLLECTION

Weyerhaeuser Way, Federal Way, 206-661-9377

The largest collection of bonsai on public view in the western U.S., in a natural forest setting.

Other Resources

NATIONAL PARK SERVICE INFORMATION CENTER

915 2nd Ave., Suite 442, Seattle, 206-220-7460

Information on camping, hiking, reservations, and fees for Washington's national parks and forests.

WASHINGTON TOURIST INFORMATION

P.O. Box 42500, Olympia, 800-544-1800

For a traveler's guide, request extension 011.

CREDITS

The authors have made every effort to reach copyright holders of text and owners of illustrations, and wish to thank those individuals and institutions that permitted the reprinting of text or the reproduction of works in their collections. Credits not listed in the captions are provided below. References are to page numbers; the designations a, b, and c indicate position of illustrations on pages.

Text

Audubon Magazine: Excerpt from "The Nature of Things" by Donald Culross Peattie from *Audubon,* September-October, 1941.

Bellowing Ark Press: Lines from "Phases of Rainier" from *Collected Shorter Poems* by Nelson Bentley. Copyright © 1966 by Nelson Bentley.

HarperCollins: From *The Egg and I* by Betty MacDonald. Copyright © 1945 by Betty MacDonald. Renewed © 1973 by Donald C. MacDonald, Elizabeth Evans, and Joan Keil. *Treasury of American Gardens* by James M. Fitch and F. F. Rockwell. Copyright © 1956 by Harper & Brothers.

Harcourt Brace & Company: *Memories of a Catholic Girlhood* by Mary McCarthy. Copyright © 1957 by Mary McCarthy. Renewed © 1981 by Mary McCarthy.

Ludlow Music, Inc.: Excerpt from "Roll on, Columbia." Words by Woody Guthrie. Music based on "Goodnight, Irene" by Huddie Ledbetter and John A. Lomax. Copyright © 1936 (renewed) 1957 (renewed) and 1963 (renewed) Ludlow Music, Inc., New York, New York. Used by permission.

The New Press: From *Inside U. S. A.* by John Gunther. Copyright © 1946, 1947 by John Gunther. Renewed © 1947 by the Curtis Publishing Company.

Penguin Putnam, Inc.: Excerpt from *Skid Row: An Informal Portrait* by Murray Morgan. Copyright © 1951 Murray Morgan. Used by permission of Viking, a division of Penguin Putnam, Inc.

Random House, Inc.: From *Another Roadside Attraction* by Thomas Robbins. Copyright © 1971 by Thomas E. Robbins. Lines from "Meditation at Oyster River," copyright © 1960 by Beatrice Roethke, Administratrix of the Estate of Theodore Roethke. From *The Collected Poems of Theodore Roethke* by Theodore Roethke. Except from *Northwest Gateway: The Story of the Port of Seattle* by Archie Binns. Copyright © 1941 by Archie Binns. Excerpt from *Seattle* by Nard Jones. Copyright © 1972 by Nard Jones. All of the above, used by permission of Doubleday, a division of Random House, Inc.

Gary Snyder: Lines from "The Late Snow & Lumber Strike of the Summer of Fifty-Four." Copyright © 1990 by Gary Snyder. Reprinted with permission.

Sunset Publishing Corporation: Recipe for "Planked Salmon" adapted from *Sunset Magazine,* August, 1997.

University of Washington Press: From *Kenneth Callahan: Universal Voyage,* edited by Michael R. Johnson. Copyright © 1973 George Yeoman Pocock quote from *Ready All* by Gordon Newell. Copyright © 1987.

W. W. Norton & Company, Inc.: From *A River Lost: The Life and Death of the Columbia* by Blaine Harden. Copyright © 1996 by Blaine Harden. Reprinted with permission.

Walla Walla Sweet Onion Marketing Committee: Recipe for "Roasted Walla Walla Sweet Onions" by Tom Douglas of The Dahlia Lounge. Reprinted with permission.

Illustrations

AMERICA HURRAH ARCHIVE, NEW YORK: **2** Nez Perce cornhusk bag; AMON CARTER MUSEUM, FORT WORTH, TEXAS: **29a** *Scene on the Columbia River* (detail). Oil on canvas. 17⅛ x 21⅛". 1972.45; **33b** *Lewis and Clark on the Lower Columbia.* Watercolor, gouache, and graphite on paper. 1961.195; BROOKLYN MUSEUM OF ART: **18** *Mount Baker, Washington.* Oil on paper. 14¼ x 19⅝". Dick S. Ramsay Fund. 47.196; ROBERT CHAMBERLAIN: **1** *Birling,* c. 1980s.; **38a** *Tug Echo and Raft,* 1989. Watercolor; CHENEY COWLES MUSEUM/EASTERN WASHINGTON STATE HISTORICAL SOCIETY: **52** *Coulee Dam—Looking West* by Vanessa Helder, c. 1940. Watercolor on paper. 18 x 21⅞". 2585.3; CHIHULY STUDIOS, SEATTLE: **84a** *Celestial Dream Persian Set.* Blown glass. 8 x 13 x 12"; **84b** *Icicle Creek Chandelier.* Blown glass. 10 x 7 x 7'; **51b** Union Station Courthouse; CHRISTIE'S IMAGES: **15a** *Rhododendron* by Paul De Longpre. Pencil on board. 18/4 x 13⅜", CORBEL. **09** Photo Pat O'Hara; CORBIS-BETTMANN: **46** *Marcus Whitman and his party,* 1836. Artist unknown; ALFRED CURRIER: **43a** *Fields of Gold,* 1996. Oil on canvas. 18 x 36"; CYAN, INC.: **44** © 1996, 1997 Cyan, Inc. All rights reserved Riven ® Cyan, Inc.; GARDE RAIL GALLERY, SEATTLE: **81b** *Apple Picker God* by Tim Fowler, 1995. Hand-carved hardwoods. 28 x 19 x 10";

GONZAGA UNIVERSITY LIBRARY: **86c** Bing Crosby; LISA HARRIS GALLERY, SEATTLE: **5** *Red Chair* by Joel Brock, 1998. Pastel on paper. 27 x 24"; HENRY ART GALLERY, UNIVERSITY OF WASHINGTON: **26** *Pines* by Edgar Forkner, c. 1911–20. Watercolor on paper. 22 x 17⅜". Horace C. Henry Collection; LINDA HODGES GALLERY: **41** *Fish Migration* by Gaylen Hansen, 1996–97. Oil on canvas. 4 x 5'; HONOLULU ACADEMY OF ARTS: **33a** Medallion of Captain James Cook. Staffordshire Wedgwood green jasperware. 4½ x 3½". Gift of the Estate of Molly Purdy, 1951. 1162.1; KELLY/MOONEY PHOTOGRAPHY: **70a**; STEVEN MASLACH: **85a** *Untitled* by Steven Maslach. 14 cast glass panels, each 2 x 16'. Courtesy the artist; MYERSON & NOWINSKI ART ASSOCIATES: **78a** *Host of Listeners* by Robert Helm, 1997. Oil on panel with wood inlay. 27 x 35 x 2½"; MUSEUM OF HISTORY AND INDUSTRY, SEATTLE: **8** *Untitled* by Alice Samson, c. 1907. Oil on canvas. 24 x 34¼". **17b** Great Northern Railway train, c. early 1890s; **23** *Panoramic View of Olympic Mountains*. Oil on canvas. 30 x 59¾". Gift of Victor Denny; **34** *Battle of Seattle*. Oil on canvas. 14½ x 20¾"; 1955.921b; **37b** Train; **60a** Stump-house. Pemco Webster and Stevens Collection; **62b** Kinnear Mansion. Pemco Webster and Stevens Collection; **70b** Waterskiers; NATIONAL ARCHIVES: **53b**; NATIONAL GEOGRAPHIC IMAGE COLLECTION: **12a** Washington flag. Illustration by Marilyn Dye Smith; **12b** Goldfinch and rhododendron. Illustration by Robert E. Hynes; MARVIN OLIVER: **82b** *Facing You* by Marvin Oliver, 1997. Glass and steel. 30" h. Private collection; CAROLINE ORR: **82a** *Elk Spirit* by Caroline Orr, 1994. Cast glass with copper. 10 x 11". Collection Washington State Percent for Art program; PILCHUCK GLASS SCHOOL: **85b**; LILLIAN PITT: **31** Wishxam totem, 1995. Clay, wood, and beads. 53 x 18 x 5"; PRIVATE COLLECTION: **17a**; Paradise Inn, Rainier National Park sticker, c. 1920s–30s; © JOEL W. ROGERS: **66, 71, 77a**; SAN FRANCISCO PUBLIC LIBRARY: **16** *On the Sound* by Charles Graham, c. 1890s. Illustration from *Harper's Weekly;* **36a** *View of Seattle;* SCHOPPERT ESTATE: **83b** *Stillwater* by James G. Schoppert, 1983. Acrylic on carved red cedar. 24 x 72 x 3". Washington State Arts Commission/Skagit Valley College; SEATTLE ART MUSEUM: **30b** *T'cayas.* Soft-twined basket. Cattail leaves, bear grass, red cedar bark. 8 x 10¼". Gift of John H. Hauberg. 86.91; **48** *Northwest Landscape* by Kenneth Callahan, 1934. Oil on board. 34 x 47". Eugene Fuller Memorial Collection. 34.137; **49a** *Forms Follow Man* by Mark Tobey, 1934. Tempera on cardboard. 20¾ x 23¾". Eugene Fuller Memorial Collection.

50.90; **49b** *Message* by Morris Graves, 1943. Ink and tempera on paper. 27½ x 53". Gift of Marion Willard Johnson. 83.209; **78b** *Obos I* by George Tsutakawa, 1956. Teak. 23¼ x 9¾". Gift of Seattle Art Museum Guild. 79.7; **80b** *Milltown Exit* by Fay Jones, 1984. Acrylic on canvas. 65½ x 52¾". Gift of the Pacific Northwest Art Council. 84.168; **81a** *The Studio* by Jacob Lawrence, 1977. Gouache on paper. 30 x 22". Partial gift of Gull Industries; John H. and Ann Hauberg; Links, Seattle; and gift by exchange from the Estate of Mark Tobey. 90.27; SECRETARY OF STATE: **12** Washington state seal; SMITHSONIAN INSTITUTION, ARCHIVES OF AMERICAN GARDENS: **64**; STAGEIMAGE: **76** Photo Ron Scherl; **77b** Photo Julie Lemberger; **88** Photo Steve J. Sherman; GAIL TREMBLAY: **83** *Star Burst,* 1990. Mixed media, metals, metallic yarns. 47 x 42 x 2"; UNIVERSITY OF WASHINGTON LIBRARIES: **11** "The Apple Family" postcard; **32** *A View in Coal Harbour;* **59** Cover of *The Four Hour Day;* WASHINGTON STATE HISTORICAL SOCIETY, TACOMA: **20** *Mount Rainier* by Lionel E. Salmon, 1938. Oil on canvas. 43¾ x 55¾"; **30b** Beaded bags. 9¼ x 8½"; **35a** Mrs. Thomas Russell; **35b** Swivel-mounted gun; **36b** Prospector, 1897; **38b** *Durable Douglas Fir,* **40a** Poster; **42** "Giant Grapes"; **47** Arboreal homestead; **50a** Map; **50b** Brochure cover; **53a** Diablo Dam, 1929; **58a** Labor union pin; **58b** *Seattle, Wash., The Great Depression.* Watercolor on paper. 11½ x 12½"; F. STUART WESTMORLAND: **86b** Coffee sign, Pike Place; WESTSTOCK: **65a** Steve Solum; **86a** Stonehenge. Photo Terry Donnelly; **87b** Whidbey Island. Photo Tim Heneghan; **87c** Petrified wood. Photo Steve Solum; WING LUKE ASIAN MUSEUM: **79** *Boats in the Harbor* by Sumio Arima, 1923. Oil on canvas. Collection of the Arima Family. WILLIAM P. WRIGHT: **87a** *Seattle George* by Buster Simpson. Aluminum. 28' h.

Acknowledgments

Walking Stick Press wishes to thank our project staff: Miriam Lewis, Joanna Lynch, Thérèse Martin, Laurie Donaldson, Inga Lewin, Kristi Hein, and Mark Woodworth.

For other assistance with *Washington,* we are especially grateful to: Laurel Anderson/Photosynthesis, Cynthia Bayley, Greg Bell of the Tacoma Art Museum, Chihuly Studios, Regina Hackett of the *Seattle Post-Intelligencer,* Jan Hughes, Jens Lund, Marge Levy at Pilchuck Glass School, Elaine Miller at the Washington State Historical Society, Lillian Pitt, Seattle Art Museum, Melissa Serdy at Corbis/Bettmann, Dave Stevenson, and Cathy Van Veen of Weststock.